Effective Communication

Knowledge and Skills for Social Care Workers series

The Knowledge and Skills for Social Care Workers series features accessible open learning workbooks which tackle a range of key subjects relevant to people working with adults in residential or domiciliary settings. Not just a source of guidance, these workbooks are also designed to meet the requirements of Health and Social Care (Adults) NVQ Level 3, with interactive exercises to develop practice.

other books in the series

Reflecting On and Developing Your Practice
A Workbook for Social Care Workers
Suzan Collins
ISBN 978 1 84310 930 3

Safeguarding Adults
A Workbook for Social Care Workers
Suzan Collins
ISBN 978 1 84310 928 0

Health and Safety
A Workbook for Social Care Workers
Suzan Collins
ISBN 978 1 84310 929 7

Effective Communication

A Workbook for Social Care Workers

Suzan Collins

Jessica Kingsley Publishers
London and Philadelphia

First published in 2009
by Jessica Kingsley Publishers
116 Pentonville Road
London N1 9JB, UK
and
400 Market Street, Suite 400
Philadelphia, PA 19106, USA

www.jkp.com

Library of Congress Cataloging in Publication Data
A CIP catalog record for this book is available from the Library of Congress

British Library Cataloguing in Publication Data
A CIP catalogue record for this book is available from the British Library

Marlow's Hierarchy of Needs, p.78: all reasonable efforts to trace the copyright holder have been made, and any enquiries should be addressed to the publisher.

ISBN 978 1 84310 927 3

Printed and bound in Great Britain by
Printwise (Haverhill) Ltd, Suffolk

Acknowledgement

Lee Nevill (Lowestoft College) for his assistance and support

This workbook meets the requirements of the following standards, guidance and qualifications

Care Quality Commission (CQC)
Care Home for Adults Standard 33.9
Domiciliary Care Standard Appendix D

General Social Care Council (GSCC)
Code of Practice Standard 2

National Vocational Qualification in Health and Social Care
NVQ HSC Level 3, Unit 31

Skills for Care (SfC)
Common Induction Standard 4

Contents

Introduction	9
Why We Need to be Able to Communicate	12
Communication within your Team, Families and Outside Agencies	15
Capacity to Make a Decision	17
Communicating with an Individual	18
Communication Profile or Communication Passport	20
Problems in Communication	23
The Different Ways We Communicate	25
Providing Opportunities to Communicate	29
Communication Cycle	30
Listening Skills	31
Factors Affecting Communication	35
Visual Reminders	40
Stimulation	41
Feelings, Emotions and Relationships	42
Objects of Reference	44
Using Photographs	46
Alternative Ways of Communicating	55
Making Choices	65
Personal Space	66
Body Language	68
Supporting Various Kinds of Service Users	71
Sensitive and Complex Issues	75

Human Growth and Development 78

Recording and Reporting 88

Confidentiality 91

Data Protection Act 1998 94

Access of Health Records Act 1990 95

Self-Assessment Tool 96

Certificate 98

Knowledge Specification Chart 100

Legislation and Useful Websites 103

References 107

Introduction

Everybody can communicate, but not always in the way you are used to. This workbook has been devised to enable you to learn how to communicate effectively, using a variety of methods and trying different tools to communicate with people.

This workbook has been written for staff, carers and family members, in fact anyone who supports or knows someone with different communication skills.

It is not always possible for staff to be taken off the rota to attend a training course and so this workbook has been devised. It uses a variety of training methods:

- reading passages where you will expand your knowledge

- completing exercises

- completing a self-assessment tool which shows you the knowledge you now have

As a social care worker, you have to work to certain standards, which are set out by various professional bodies. This workbook links to several standards and if you are not familiar with them, here is a brief explanation of each one.

Skills for Care (SfC) has a set of standards called Common Induction Standards and all new staff in the care sector (except those who are supporting people with learning disabilities) have to complete these with their manager within three months of being in post. This workbook meets the requirements of Standard 4.

Care Quality Commission (CQC) took over the work of the Commission for Social Care Inspection (CSCI) on 1 April 2009 (it also took over the work of the Healthcare Commission and the Mental Health Act Commission). The CQC has sets of standards for you and your workplace to meet. There are different sets of standards and it will depend on where you work as to which standards you need to work to. If you are unsure please ask your manager. This workbook meets the requirements of Care Homes for Adults Standard 33.9 (Department of Health 2003) and Domiciliary Care Standard 11 Appendix D (Department of Health 2000).

Care Home for Adults Standard 33.9:

> There are staff on duty at all times who can communicate with service users in their first language including sign; and have skills in other methods relevant to service users' needs (e.g. block alphabet, Braille, finger spelling, Makaton, total communication, manual deafblind language, moon, personal symbols).

Domiciliary Care Standard 11:

> Training should also include communication skills (with the people you support).

General Social Care Council (GSCC) has a Code of Practice with six standards in it that reflect good practice. This workbook meets the requirements of Standard 2. Towards the end of the workbook you will be asked to fill in a self-assessment questionnaire on what you have learned from completing this workbook. Once you have done this your Manager or Trainer will complete the certificate and give it back to you.

NVQ HSC is a *National Vocational Qualification in Health and Social Care*.

This workbook has been written first and foremost to enable effective communication between people and to enable staff to complete 'communication' training, without leaving the workplace.

If you are thinking about doing or working towards an NVQ Level 3 in Health and Social Care, you will find that this workbook is a great help to you.

When you have registered for an NVQ, you will be allocated an NVQ Assessor who will arrange to observe you in the workplace and guide you through your NVQ award. This guidance will involve devising action plans, which will consist of things like:

- Writing an account of how you did something in the workplace, e.g. helping someone to make a cup of tea, providing support to a service user with his/her training programme, identifying risks, supporting someone to go to the shops etc. This is called a 'self-reflective account' (SRA).

- Asking others to write an account of what you have done. This is called a 'witness report' (WR).

- Completing a set of questions which is called 'the knowledge specification'. This is where you can use this workbook for reference.

This workbook covers all the knowledge specification requirements for the NVQ Unit 31 'Positive effective communication for and about individuals', which can be found towards the end of this workbook (see Knowledge Specification Chart).

I hope that you find this a useful workbook and wish you well in your career.

This workbook can be:

- read straight through from front to back
- read from front to back, answering the questions as you go, and these can be used as evidence towards the NVQ Unit 31
- used as a reference book.

In this workbook I have referred to the people you support as 'individuals', 'service users' or 'he/him', rather than continually writing he/she, him/her.

Name of Learner:. . . . . Date: . . . .

Signature of Learner:. . . . .

Name of Manager or Trainer: . . . .

Signature of Manager or Trainer: . . . . Date: . . . .

Workplace address or name of organization:

. . . .

. . . .

. . . .

. . . .

Why We Need to be Able to Communicate

We need to be able to communicate in order to share:

- information

- ideas

- feelings.

The CQC requirements on communication were described in the Introduction.

Each individual you support will have his own style and level of communication. Some will be very good at talking, others not very good at talking, or not able to talk at all, some will be good at getting their message across by writing notes or letters, others will use sign language, others will point to what they want. Others will be good at listening and others may not, some will use their body language to communicate, e.g. smiling to show they are happy or folding their arms or hands on hips to show they are annoyed.

Your friends and family will also have their own style and level of communication.

✍ Think of a friend and also a family member, and write here what their own style and level of communication is:

. . . .

. . . .

. . . .

. . . .

Individuals who are visually impaired, hard of hearing or deaf, or who have suffered a stroke, have dementia or a learning disability, may have their own style of communication.

✑ If you are a paid carer or support worker, please have a look at your job description. What does it say in terms of communication?

. . . .

. . . .

. . . .

. . . .

Maybe it says something like:

- Communicate with...
- Inform...
- Record...
- Report...

Your job description will also say that you need to promote these *values*: choice, rights, respect, dignity, independence, confidentiality, identity and individuality.

✑ How can you do this if you do not know how the individual is communicating to or with you?

. . . .

. . . .

. . . .

. . . .

✍ Have a look at your organization's policy on *equal opportunities*. How can you use this when communicating and/or writing records?

. . . .

. . . .

. . . .

. . . .

Is information presented in an accessible format, e.g. are images used to break down information?   Yes/No

To be able to support individuals you need to consider:

- why individuals want to communicate

- how the individual communicates with others

- how you as staff communicate with the individual

- understand that all behaviour is a form of communication.

Why do you need to do this? The answer is clear...

If you do not do this, you could be speaking a foreign language to each other, which causes frustration or avoiding talking because you cannot understand each other and neither of you will get your message across.

This means that the service users are unable to have control over the most basic things in life, such as having a cup of tea and choosing where they want to drink it etc.

But, before you go any further, it is important for you to consider how communication works within the team, with families, and with outside agencies. If the communication is not effective within and between these groups, then the communication with the service users will not be right.

Communication within your Team, Families and Outside Agencies

✍ Please answer the following questions about your team, families and outside agencies.

The team you work in	Yes/No
Are you informed of what you need to do and when you need to do it?	
Are you informed of changes to care plans or individuals' needs?	
Are you asked for your opinion?	
Do people in your team talk to each other?	
Do some talk more than others?	
Do you all remember each other's names?	
Do you all respect each other?	
Do you all listen to each other?	
Are verbal or written messages passed on?	
Does everyone write up the care plans at the end of each shift?	
Is there someone who always forgets to complete his write-up?	
Do any of your colleagues have poor writing skills?	
Are tasks, activities and appointments written in the dairy?	
If you tell a member of the team something in confidence, does it remain confidential?	

Families	Yes/No
Is there effective communication between the team and the families?	
Are members of the family asked for their opinion?	
Do members of the family want to be involved in the care and support?	
Are the people you support supported to keep in touch with family?	
Outside agencies	
Is there effective communication between the team and outside agencies?	
Is there effective communication between the families and outside agencies?	
Are the team informed of any changes to the individual's care needs or plans?	

Now you have completed the three exercises, would you say that the communication is effective?   Yes/No

✍ If you answered 'No' to any of these, what are the consequences?

For the individual:. . . . .

. . . .

For the family:. . . . .

. . . .

For your team:. . . . .

. . . .

For outside agencies:. . . . .

. . . .

Capacity to Make a Decision

Everyone has a right to make their own choices in life and this includes the people you support.

The Mental Capacity Act 2005 states that we must assume everyone can make a decision unless proved otherwise. You should bear the following in mind:

- You must not assume a person cannot make a decision.

- You should assume a person can make a decision unless proved otherwise.

- A person should not be treated as incapable of making a decision because his decision may seem unwise.

- Always do things for people without capacity in their best interest.

- Before doing something to someone or making a decision on that person's behalf, consider whether the outcome could be achieved in a less restrictive way.

- Decisions can be both small (having a cup of tea or coffee) and large (moving from home into a residential service).

A person can make a decision if he is able to:

- understand information given to him

- retain the information long enough to be able to make the decision

- weigh up the information available to make the decision

- communicate his decision: this could be by talking, using sign language or even simple movements.

Communicating with an Individual

How do you know how to communicate with the service user and how the individual communicates with you and others?

First and foremost, find out how the individual wishes to be addressed, e.g. Mr, Mrs, Miss, Ms, Jo, Bert and so on. This is very important as you should always say the person's name at the start of a conversation. This informs the person you are speaking to him, gets his attention, and shows respect. Please be aware that in some cultures it is disrespectful to call someone by his first name if you do not know that person well.

To communicate you need to get to know the individual, listen to what the person is saying or telling you and you need to observe the body language also. How many times have you said 'I'm fine' but really you are very tired and the way you hold your body (slouching) tells people this.

If you are meeting a service user for the first time, you can find out his preferred method of communication by asking him a question, e.g. 'How are you?' Start by talking in English and if the individual responds then you can carry on. Watch his body language and his facial expression as this will show if you are talking at the right speed and level.

If the individual does not respond, you will need to consider other methods. If someone is deaf, can he lipread, and if he can lipread does he want to lipread long messages from your lips or have them written down? If he can read, writing down the messages will be clearer.

For individuals whose first language is not English, they may want an interpreter, or messages written down or signed, or to be shown pictures. You have to find out their preferred method of communication so you can discuss their needs. A family member may want to interpret for the individual: you will need to ensure that he is interpreting the exact words you want him to and not adding some of his own.

Another way of finding out is to observe the individual in the company of others. Is he verbally communicating? Is he hearing what the other person is saying? What is his body language like? Is it tight or open?

You could also look in the individual's records to find out how the individual communicates. Every service user may have a care plan and it may be recorded there how the individual prefers to communicate. In some services individuals have a communication profile (some call it a communication passport) for recording how the individual communicates.

 Please ask your manager what is in place to inform you on how the individual communicates.

The care plan, profile or passport (a sample is in the next section) will also tell you if the individual has had a speech assessment. If he has not, or it is over five years old, ask your manager to arrange for the individual to be referred for the assessment by a speech therapist.

Before accessing the care plan, please look at your policy on accessing records. It will inform you on who can access the records. It will include asking the individual if you can access his records and may say that if the individual is unable to give his consent, there will be a named person who can give you permission to access his records; this could be a family member or a named carer etc.

Communication Profile or Communication Passport

A communication profile or communication passport will inform staff on how the service user communicates with others and wishes to be communicated with. It also enables consistency between staff, as all staff will be communicating the same way with the individual. The profile or passport will need to be updated regularly. This tool can be used for all individuals, e.g. people with a learning disability or physical disability, people who have had a stroke, those who are deaf or blind etc.

Here is an example of a profile or passport.

Name of individual:. . . . .

Name of person completing the form: . . . .

I like to be called: . . . .

I communicate by:. . . . .

I like you to communicate with me by:. . . . .

I initiate communication by: . . . .

I can speak	Yes/No, a little, a lot
I can read	Yes/No, a little, a lot
I can write	Yes/No, a little, a lot
I can write my name	Yes/No, a little, a lot
I can sign my name (signature)	Yes/No, a little, a lot
I can copy words/writing	Yes/No, a little, a lot

I can use the telephone (to make a call in or out)   Yes/No, a little, a lot

I can answer the telephone and say 'Hello'   Yes/No, a little, a lot

I may not be able to communicate with you when: . . . .

. . . .

I can use/understand Makaton   Yes/No, a little, a lot

I can use/understand BSL   Yes/No, a little, a lot

I can use any of these to communicate:

    video   Yes/No

    photographs   Yes/No

    talking photo albums   Yes/No

    pictures   Yes/No

I can tell the time   Yes/No

I can understand what is in a picture or photograph   Yes/No

I can understand what is on the TV   Yes/No

I like touch   Yes/No

I like to be touched but only on my arms or on my hands or feet
when they are being massaged   Yes/No

I can tell you if I am unhappy. I do this by: . . . .

. . . .

I do/do not need to use communication tools. If I do these are: . . . .

. . . .

I will not communicate with you when: . . . .

. . . .

When I am happy or like something I will show you by:. . . . .

. . . .

When I am unhappy, or do not like something I will show you by:. . . . .

. . . .

I have/have not had a hearing assessment in the last 2 years

Delete appropriately

The date of my last hearing assessment: . . . .

I have/have not had a speech assessment in the last 5 years

Delete appropriately

The date of my last speech assessment:. . . . .

I have/have not had a communication assessment in the last 5 years

Delete appropriately

The date of my last communication assessment:. . . . .

I have/have not had an eye test in the last 2 years   Delete appropriately

The date of my last eye test: . . . .

I do/do not wear glasses   Delete appropriately

If I wear glasses I need to wear them all the time/just for reading

Delete appropriately

I have got glasses, which I should wear but choose not to   Yes/No

Date the profile developed:. . . . .

Date of when profile will be reviewed: . . . .

Problems in Communication

If individuals are not communicating in a way you can understand, then the individuals will not be able to:

- have a conversation (something you do endless times a day)
- make choices in what they need and want
- express and fight for their rights
- access community facilities, including paid work (if applicable)
- become independent or maintain independence (doing things for themselves, no matter how small or large)
- express compliments, give comments and make a complaint.

Two-way communication is important and can be effective only when both parties are involved. If the conversation is one way the other person:

- may think he is being devalued
- may not feel part of the conversation
- may not listen to you or take on board what you are saying.

There is a need to stop and listen to service users to enable each person to have a say in his choices in life.

If you are unable to know what the service user would like, the individual could feel isolated. This isolation can lead to frustration and some may have no alternative but to use behaviour to show that they want to tell you something (challenging behaviour).

Challenging behaviour is a form of communication, i.e. expressing what someone wants through behaviour, and staff need to turn this challenging behaviour into positive communication. Challenging behaviour can also happen if staff are not consistent in their approach when communicating with the individual, e.g. if one staff member uses pictures and another staff member uses verbal communication, this can confuse the individual especially if he understands pictures and not the spoken word. If he is able to understand the spoken word and a staff member uses pictures he may feel belittled by this.

You will need to be able to help and support each individual to find a positive way of communicating and expressing his needs and this workbook will give you plenty of ideas.

If the individual is not communicating in the way you know, then he will lose the power and control over his own life and become reliant on you. It is important to enable the individual to take control of his life and make his own decisions.

The level of understanding each individual may have and the ability to respond will be different for each individual: what works for one may not work for another.

It is important when communicating that you recognize each person's unique way of communicating and do not discriminate against anyone, regardless of culture, religion, ability, level of communication etc.

There are many different cultures and beliefs and these must not infringe on others who live in the residential service.

You are sitting at the dining table supporting someone with his breakfast. Your colleague comes to the table with another person. After sitting down, your colleague automatically starts pouring cereal into a bowl for the person without asking him what he would like. When you mention it, she says that he cannot speak so she made the decision for him.

What are your thoughts on this and what should you do?

. . . .

. . . .

. . . .

. . . .

The Different Ways We Communicate

Here are some examples of the ways we communicate with one another:

- facial expression
- talking
- pointing
- gesturing
- sounds
- writing
- drawing
- silence

- laughing, crying
- the way we dress
- touch
- body language
- email, fax
- computers
- telephone.

To get you thinking about how communication and expressing your needs is important to you, please complete the following exercises:

✎ You are on duty and someone asks your opinion. Before you can answer, another member of staff answers for you. How would you feel?

. . . .

. . . .

. . . .

. . . .

✍ Think of a place abroad that you have visited where you didn't know the language, currency or where you were going. How did you manage to work out the currency or go where you wanted to go? How did you feel?

. . . .

. . . .

. . . .

. . . .

✍ Imagine you go shopping every week with your friend, partner or mum and every week you pass the same clothes shop and notice an item in the window that you would really like. You cannot tell your friend, partner or mum as you cannot speak. How would you feel?

. . . .

. . . .

. . . .

. . . .

✍ What could you do about this (bearing in mind you cannot speak)?

. . . .

. . . .

. . . .

. . . .

✍ One day your friend, partner or mum takes you into the shop and he/she buys you an item of clothing but it's not the one you wanted. How do you feel?

. . . .

. . . .

. . . .

. . . .

✍ What can you do about this (bearing in mind you cannot speak)?

. . . .

. . . .

. . . .

. . . .

Your feelings will be the same as the service user may feel every day. You will need to work out a communication system for the service user to use so he can express his needs.

If the individual cannot speak you may want to make choices for him. Please do not do this as this is disrespectful and hurtful to the person.

We communicate for the following reasons:

- to ask for something

- to express an opinion or point of view

- to find out things

- to reveal parts of yourself

- to have a conversation with others, e.g. friends, neighbours, animals, professionals.

The following are examples of what can motivate us to communicate:

- expressing an opinion

- responding to requests

- making requests

- wanting to know something

- wanting to be engaged in conversation (makes you feel valued and wanted).

Providing Opportunities to Communicate

Policies, procedures, risk assessments and many other items may be written in text and the individual may not understand it. If information is in an accessible format, the individual will be able to comprehend it and comment on it. This can be achieved by using pictures, photographs etc. and this will be covered later on in the workbook.

When you are having a conversation it is better to ask 'open' questions rather than 'closed' questions. Closed questions are used to gain a specific piece of information, often in only one word, whereas open questions can encourage a more general and possibly lengthy reply.

- *Closed question*: 'Are you OK?' 'Yes'.

- *Open question*: 'How are you today?' 'I am fine, thank you, how are you?'

Here are some tips to help you communicate with your service users:

- Focus on the individual.

- Use short sentences.

- Talk about things that interest the individual.

- If you have difficulty understanding the individual, look at his body language or ask for help.

- Encourage people who have the same interest to meet and talk about them.

- Encourage the individual to be involved in tasks and activities.

- Sometimes it is nice to 'job-share', i.e. help each other or make the other person a cup of tea etc.

For individuals who have dementia, it may take time for the brain to process the information and therefore the individual may be better at responding to closed questions than open ones.

Communication Cycle

Having a cycle of communication enables effective communication and as you will see from the diagram, there are four components: inform, invite, listen and acknowledge.

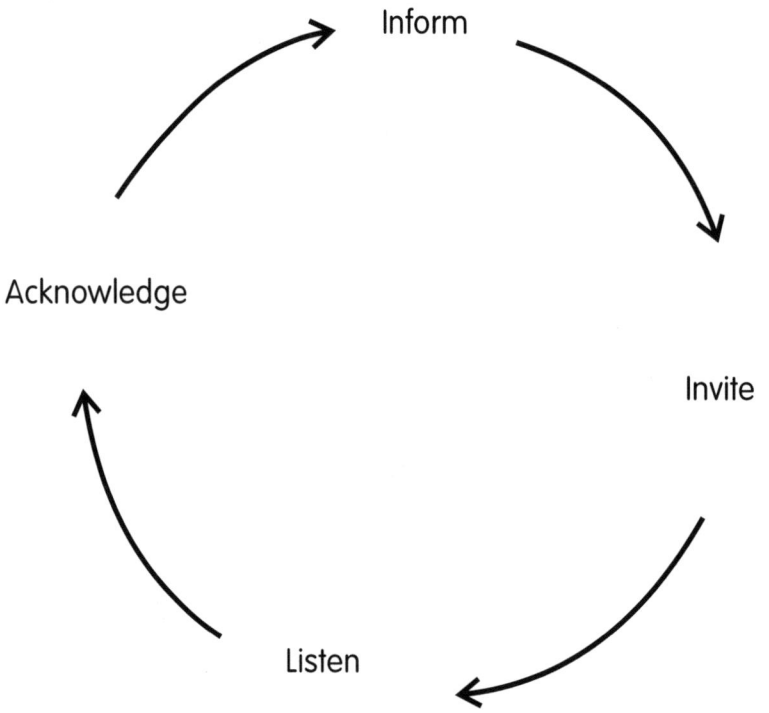

- *Inform*: this is where the conversation starts by asking an open question.

- *Invite*: this is where you wait for a response.

- *Listen*: it is important to listen as you need to hear what was said in order to continue the conversation.

- *Acknowledge*: this is important because it demonstrates that you are listening.

Listening Skills

Active listening involves tuning into emotions and the feeling behind the words as well as just the words themselves.

FACIAL EXPRESSION

Your facial expression will show the service user whether you have been listening or not.

Watch the individual's facial expression when communicating with him as this can let you know if he has understood what you have said. If the face is strained or he is looking at you with a blank stare, this could be a sign that he has not understood you.

Your beliefs about a person may affect your ability to listen. An example of this is that if you think the person is boring, the listening will become more of a struggle, and your facial expression will show this.

Professor Albert Mehrabian has pioneered the understanding of communications since the 1960s. He established this classic statistic for the effectiveness of spoken communications:

- 7% of meaning is in the words that are spoken.
- 38% of meaning is paralinguistic (the way that the words are said).
- 55% of meaning is in facial expression.

(Mehrabian 1960)

HOW TO LISTEN

- Lean towards the individual when he is speaking.

- Nod your head at appropriate times.

- Ask questions when the individual has finished speaking.

- Do not interrupt the individual.

- Maintain eye contact, but do not stare.

- Do not fidget, sit still.

- Try to relax.

- Have open body language (e.g. don't fold your arms; try placing your hands in your lap).

TIME TO LISTEN

- Give sufficient time for the individual to understand the content of what you have said.

- You could ask open questions to find out if he has understood you.

- Sometimes when you are listening you may mirror what the talker is doing, e.g. if he scratches his head you may automatically scratch yours.

- Remember that in some cultures people remain still and may look away while the person is talking, and this shows they are listening. If you do not wait for the person to finish talking and talk over someone, then this is seen as being disrespectful.

Hearing is a sense many are likely to have.

Listening is a skill that needs to be developed.

Ask a colleague or a friend to help you with this listening exercise.

Your friend or colleague should talk to you for a few minutes and tell you what he/she did last night.

After a few minutes your friend or colleague will stop talking.

Repeat back what he/she told you and ask if this is correct.

Was it correct? Yes/No

Ask how he/she knew you were listening and write it down here:

. . . .

. . . .

. . . .

. . . .

HOW TO COMMUNICATE AT THE RIGHT LEVEL

If you are both sitting down, make sure the height of the chairs is the same. If one chair is higher than the other, this will make the person on the lower chair feel intimidated and anxious and he may not feel comfortable communicating.

If you are having a conversation with a service user who is in a wheelchair or in bed, then come down to his height.

Ask a colleague or a friend to help you with this exercise.

Sit yourself on a chair and ask the colleague or friend to stand by you and have a conversation between yourselves. How did you feel?

. . . .

. . . .

. . . .

. . . .

THINGS TO REMEMBER WHEN COMMUNICATING WITH SOMEONE

- Listen to what the person is saying.

- Do not interrupt: you cannot listen and talk at the same time.

- Do not patronize: if you are talking to an adult then speak to him as an adult.

- Talk to the service user, not the staff providing support, e.g. don't say 'Does Tony want to go out?' You could ask Tony if he would like to go out and if he cannot speak, watch his facial expression. If he wants to go out, he will show you by smiling and/or raising his eyebrows etc.

- Interpret what the person is saying, both verbally and in body language.

- Look into the person's eyes: someone wearing glasses (especially dark glasses) can put off a person wanting to talk to him. If the individual cannot see the other person's eyes, this can bring on a feeling of insecurity or of being scared. (We can lose a lot of understanding if we are unable to see facial expressions: this will be covered in more detail later.)

- Ask questions so both of you will know if you have understood each other.

- Check the person's facial expression: if it is showing that he has not understood you, try saying it again but reword it.

Factors Affecting Communication

The service user's ability to communicate may be affected in the following ways. *The individual*:

- may be blind and cannot find the person he wants to speak to

- may have heard staff say, 'I know what he needs, I don't need to ask. I'll buy it for him on my next day off,' so he may not bother voicing an opinion

- may not have the ability or skill to speak

- may be female and belongs to a culture that does not allow females to talk, or as a child the individual was not allowed to speak in front of the parents

- may not have been asked for his opinion

- might not speak English as his first language

- may have a different accent from yours.

Staff members may affect communication in the following ways:

- Staff members may not have received training on alternative communication and are unable to interpret what the service user is communicating.

- Staff members may not have adapted their communication to suit the individual.

- The service user may feel intimidated by staff members, especially if their build is large or muscular and the staff members stand too close to the individual.

- Past experience may have shown that staff did not listen to the service user's views or his attempts to communicate.

- High service user to staff ratio may hinder communication.

- The service user cannot communicate verbally and no one has thought about using different tools to aid communication such as photographs or pictures.

Difficulty in hearing can affect communication.

- Check whether the individual has had a recent hearing test.

- The service user could be deaf and has not learnt to sign, or the staff have not been trained in British Sign Language (BSL).

- If the service user wears a hearing aid, he may not have been supported and encouraged to wear it, or the batteries may have run out.

- The individual may have a problem hearing but staff or relatives may be unaware of this.

- Does the service user require products that he can use in his home and take with him when he goes on holiday, for example:

    ◦ a visual/audio smoke detector

    ◦ door knock signaller

    ◦ telephone amplifier.

    ◦ A telecommunications device for the deaf (TDD) can change letters typed on a keyboard into beeps, which can be transmitted over the telephone line.

Lack of understanding and *emotional factors* can affect communication. The service user:

- may not be able to understand what is being said and therefore may feel staff are speaking a foreign language

- may be able to speak but not comprehend what is being said

- may be too upset or distressed to talk

- may be in pain, which may prevent him/her from wanting to communicate.

- may not understand complicated words, e.g. a GP may use complicated words when telling an individual what his problem is. The individual does not understand, but will have to accept what the GP has said; after all, he is the expert! This is a negative application of what French and Raven (1960) called 'Expert Power'.

ENVIRONMENTAL FACTORS

It is rare that we communicate well in a place that we do not like or feel unsafe in. Therefore you need to ensure that where the person is communicating is safe. You will need to consider various environmental factors.

Does the service user wish to discuss something confidential or private? If he does then a private area where you both will not be disturbed would need to be used. Ensure the room is not noisy, e.g. the radio or TV is not on or not on too loud.

It can be difficult to communicate in rooms which are spacious, or have high ceilings or walls that have been painted in loud colours.

Good lighting is needed so you can both see each other. Ensure the sun is not shining through the window and obscuring the individual's vision.

Good air circulation and temperature are important: ensure the room is not too hot or too cold. We can feel more stressed when we are hot. If the individual is stressed, find a cooler place.

Check that chairs or settees are comfortable for the individual and yourself.

 Do you support an individual who:

Finds the layout of the building confusing?	Yes/No
Goes through the wrong door?	Yes/No
Puts items in the wrong cupboard?	Yes/No
Puts things in the top part of the fridge when they should be in the bottom part, the freezer?	Yes/No

This could be for many reasons, one being that all the doors may be the same colour and texture, and therefore confusing.

Here are a few ideas, especially when service users are visually impaired:

- Painting each door in a different colour and/or making it a different texture can enable individuals to identify which door to go through, or to open if it is a cupboard.

- Painting the door frame (architrave) a different colour to the walls helps to make the door stand out from the walls.

- Painting the edge of the door (stile) in a different colour to the rest of the door helps to show when it is open: the individual will see this different colour on the edge and know it is open.

- Having a wooden picture rail at waist height (dado rail) which, as it gets near an opening or door, has studs on it which can inform the individual that he is walking towards an opening or door.

- Having different carpets with different textures can help service users to know which room they are in.

OTHER FACTORS AFFECTING COMMUNICATION

The service user may have *low self-esteem* or may be lacking in confidence, e.g. if he has a continence problem or wears a catheter.

If the service user wears *glasses* he may not have been supported or encouraged to wear them, or to clean them. An individual may have difficulty in seeing but staff might be unaware of this. Optician appointments should be at least every two years. Do you know if the individual has had a recent eye test? Is the optician using different communication tools for the individual to tell him/her about any sight problems?

Sometimes we use *idiomatic phrases*, for example when we are having a joke with someone we may say 'I was pulling your leg', but some individuals might find this confusing.

Service users may experience *poor communications from others*, e.g. outside agencies or family, or if information is not presented in an *accessible format*, e.g. images are not used to break down information.

Q: How might the service user feel if communication was only one way?

A: Talked down to or not feeling engaged: the service user may not listen or take on board what you are saying.

It is very important that these barriers are reduced. If they are not, you and the service user will have difficulty understanding each other. You need to ensure that the individual has the right tools to communicate and to understand what is being said. If he has not got these tools then he will not be able to communicate with you and vice versa, thus resulting in a breakdown of a professional relationship.

Q: You are a carer and you are late for your next visit, which is to Mrs Smith, who is deaf. How do you get a message to Mrs Smith to say you will be a little late?

A: You could send Mrs Smith a text message or telephone a hearing friend who lives nearby and can pass on a message. Please consider the best option based on your knowledge of her circumstances, and remember not notifying her is unacceptable.

Another factor to consider is *how many people* to communicate with. Some people may prefer to communicate with only one person at a time as this means that you only have to watch one person's facial expression, body language and mood. This is a lot easier than watching the facial expression, body language and mood of six people.

Feelings are also important. Expressing *feelings and emotions* can be different from one culture to another. If we feel good about ourselves we are more ready to communicate. Sometimes wearing the clothes that make us feel good or wearing a favourite perfume or aftershave can help.

Exercise is good too and this does not necessarily mean going to a gym: a walk will make you feel good too. Or you can sit in a chair and do arm exercises or circular ankle exercises.

Making assumptions can lead to poor or no communication. For example, if you assume from someone's appearance that he is going to cause trouble then you will have this image in your head and may become defensive approaching him or having a conversation with him.

TIME

Time is a misconception with some service users. To say 'in a minute' does not mean anything to someone who cannot tell the time, cannot count to 60 or is not wearing a watch. You could point to a number on the clock and say 'When the hand gets to here we will…' or use a cuckoo clock, i.e. 'When the cuckoo comes out we will…' or an egg timer or alarm clock.

Visual Reminders

We can all forget things at times and to jog our memory, we may put reminders in place:

- putting the shopping list next to your purse or car keys to remind you to go shopping

- placing items that you need to take to work tomorrow by the front door

- looking at your diary for the date and/or what you need to do tomorrow

- consulting the calendar for the day's date or to see when it is someone's birthday.

Sometimes service users cannot comprehend a calendar but would like to know when they are going to the cinema, out for a meal or to meet friends. You could use a piece of paper and write down each day from today until the day of the appointment. Then ask the individual to cross the date off each night when he goes to bed.

If the service user has dementia and relies on his diary to remind him what he did yesterday, you could also consider using it to record when the use-by date of food has expired. Perhaps the tomatoes in the fridge have an expiry date: the individual may forget this and then he will have black tomatoes in the fridge. Suggest writing a little note in the diary, something like 'If I have any tomatoes left, throw them away.'

Some people who do not have a calendar or a diary may have the day, date and year on a board and change it every morning. If they are unable to change it themselves, the carer or a family member can change it.

What is in place to enable the service users you support to know what day it is?

. . . .

. . . .

. . . .

Stimulation

Everyone needs to be stimulated; if not we become bored and sometimes fall asleep. To leave a service user in a residential home sitting for hours doing nothing and then asking him if he wants a cup of tea is not good practice. You should be communicating and interacting with individuals regularly and naturally taking an interest in their interests and hobbies, encouraging them and helping them to do things around the house, e.g. watering the plants, raking the garden, making the tea. Try to have a one-to-one session where you and the person have time to discuss anything the individual wants to.

People living in their own homes may have a variety of people to communicate with and some may have none. You may be their only source of contact and the service user may want to talk to you all the time you are there supporting him, or he may not feel like talking at all. When you arrive in the evening to help put someone to bed, it may be difficult for him to be in the frame of mind to want to communicate, after having no one to speak to all day.

Please be aware that while we all need to be stimulated, there are times when we like to sit and think. This is no different for the people you support. If the service user would like to sit and think while looking out of the window, ask him if he would like to look out of a window with better scenery or where there is perhaps a bird feeder in view.

Feelings, Emotions and Relationships

It is very important for service users to be able to express their *feelings*, especially if they cannot speak. You may wish to make up a board of different faces showing various *emotions*, e.g. smiling, happy, laughing, angry, worried, crying, in pain etc. This will enable the person to point to one to show what he is feeling.

If the person is not at the stage yet of using the board, then you could point to each one and watch the individual's face. When you point to the one that he is feeling, you may know this is the correct one by the person's facial expression.

To have a good conversation and for people to trust you (so they can tell you things) you need to build a good *relationship* with the service user and vice versa.

You need to:

- be patient

- listen

- ask questions effectively

- maintain confidentiality

- establish trust and rapport.

It is more likely that you will build a relationship with an individual if you are doing things together so that you learn or maintain the individual's skills at the same time. You will need to make sure that the individual is not the one who has to fetch and carry, i.e. go for this, go for that. There can be a tendency to give all the horrible bits of a job to an individual, e.g. you are peeling the potatoes, you ask the individual to go and put the peel in the bin, you later mash the potatoes (which is the fun part) while the individual stands watching.

Service users who experience difficulty in being understood by others may have issues with identity, self-esteem and image; they may feel incomplete or inadequate and may have a low opinion of themselves because they cannot get their message across. They may be reliant on others to decide for them and feel disempowered.

This can affect people in many ways, e.g. some may stop going out in case they meet people who they know and they will not be able to have a conversation with them.

Visually you cannot normally see if someone is deaf until you begin talking to the individual, or if the individual does something that the other person does not like, e.g. the person who is deaf ignores the other person because he cannot hear him calling, and the person who has been calling catches up and says 'Are you deaf or something, I've been calling you for ages, you stupid thing, you left your shopping by the till.' If someone is told often enough that they are stupid, then they can believe it is true and this will have a knock-on effect on a person's self-image and self-esteem.

Service users who need to wear a catheter can feel self-conscious about a bag strapped onto their leg. This could make the person feel embarrassed and not wish to socialize or communicate with anyone.

If someone has a communication board which is large, he can feel self-conscious about it. Also, the fact that he has to communicate another way other than verbally can also make him feel self-conscious and not want to communicate.

People may not talk to someone because of the difficulty in communicating; this can have a huge impact on the person's self-esteem and self-worth.

Objects of Reference

If a service user is hard of hearing or visually impaired, has very limited understanding or has dementia, how do you ask him to help with peeling the potatoes or whether he wants a bath? This is where we can use objects of reference.

An object of reference is when you show an item to give a message. Therefore if you are asking the individual to:

- peel a potato, then show a potato (give the potato to the individual to feel)

- lay the table, show cutlery

- have a bath, show the towel or the person's own bubble bath or sponge

- brush his teeth, show the toothbrush

- go to the toilet, show a toilet roll or a toilet roll holder

- sit for a foot massage, show the specific massage cream

- say if he wants a cup of tea, show the cup or box of tea bags (or jar of coffee)

- bake a cake or tart, show a mixing bowl or a rolling pin

- get ready for bed, show slippers and/or dressing gown

- go out for a walk, show shoes and/or coat

- say if he wants to play football, show the football

- tell the time, show the watch or clock.

Q: The person I support has never done any of these. How do I start doing this?

A: Everyone can do something (no matter how small or large) and we all have the right to be able to try. Please discuss with your manager first as a risk assessment may need to be in place if working in the kitchen.

When using objects of reference, it is important to remember to use the same object, with the same shape, colour and texture each time. You do not necessarily need to use exactly the same products but you must have the same sort of item to show what the task is. Therefore you may like to obtain small bottles and keep a little of the lotion, bubble bath etc. in there so the person can smell the lotion etc. and see the bottle and know what will be happening.

Do not overload the individual with conversation. Use direct words, e.g. say 'Tea?' and show the teabag container, or say 'Coffee?' and show the coffee jar. For a bath, say 'Bath?' and show bubble bath or sponge, or for a foot massage say 'Feet?' and/or point to feet and show cream.

PEELING POTATOES

If a service user has not peeled potatoes before, why not ask him if he would like to, or show him a potato and a peeler, sit at a table with him (no distractions) and give him a potato to feel. He may not have the confidence yet to try peeling a potato but the first step is feeling it. The next stage could be that the individual hands you each potato and you peel and chop them. The stage after this could be using the peeler.

It is important not to rush the individual or to push him to do things before he is ready. If the individual is not comfortable holding the peeler or peeling the potatoes, he may be happy to be with you while you do them.

You may be thinking here about personal hygiene (i.e. washing hands) and you are correct about this. However, this may put the person off as you are asking him to do two things (if the person has never done anything like this then it can be frightening for him and he may withdraw). The potato will be eventually peeled: at these early stages does it matter that the person has not washed his hands to feel the potato? If you are concerned you could put this one potato to one side and put it in the bin later.

When the individual feels a little more comfortable in sitting with you and feeling one potato, you may then ask him to wash hands. This can be done by you rubbing your hands together and pretending to wash your hands or you could both go and wash your hands at the same time.

Using Photographs

In this workbook you will learn about the use of video and photographs. Before using the video camcorder or camera you will need to gain the individual's consent and/or know your organization's policy on the use of video and taking photos. If you are unclear on this, please discuss with your manager.

Photographs have an important role to play in communicating and in many areas of service users' daily lives.

WHO IS IN THE PHOTOGRAPH?

If service users do not always remember who is in their personal photographs, you could ask them if you can put a slimline white label on the photograph to say who is in it, e.g. if the photograph is of two daughters then you could label the photo with the name of each daughter. Alternatively the names could be written on the back of the photograph. (It is preferable to write on a label first, then stick it to the back of the photo, rather than writing directly on the photo.) Please ask the individual what he prefers.

STAFF DUTY ROTA PHOTO BOARD FOR RESIDENTIAL SERVICES

Service users will want and need to know who is coming on duty and it is their right to know. Rather than wait for individuals to ask you (or get frustrated because they are unable to ask you and want to know who is coming on duty), why not devise a staff rota board and put photographs of the staff due on duty that day or night on it.

You need to choose carefully a good place to put this staff duty rota photo board, one where all the service users can see it clearly but not those who do not need to know who is on duty, e.g. repair men. This is because staff could become vulnerable if someone outside of the house knows when there is only one staff member on duty, such as some night shifts.

To start with, staff may need to change the photographs on the rota board until the service users get used to what it is, and then staff can support the individuals to change the rota photo board.

How to make a staff duty rota photo board

You will need:

- notice board (one that allows you to use drawing pins)

- dark material to cover the board

- sticky tape or Velcro

- pictures of the sun and moon or a bed.

Be careful to choose pictures that show the sun and moon or a bed and nothing else, e.g. if you look at Figure 1, it is showing a woman in a bed. When an individual is at the very early stages of learning how to use photographs, he may not associate the picture with himself but may think that the woman in the picture needs to be in bed.

Figure 1 Woman in bed

Therefore something like Figure 2 may be more acceptable.

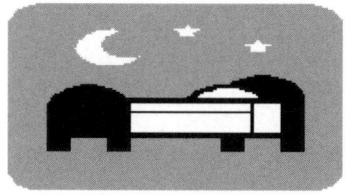

Figure 2 Empty bed

Or you may wish to use a picture of the moon (Figure 3).

 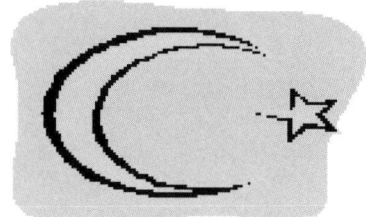

Figure 3 The moon

To start you will need a board like the one in Figure 4. You may wish to cover it with dark material such as felt: black would be too dark; perhaps a dark blue would be good, as it will show off the photographs. However, if you haven't got any material at the moment, you can do what I have done and not use any. You can always add to it in the future.

Figure 4 A notice board

Following the design in Figure 5, put sticky tape to make three rows and one column to the left.

Figure 5 A notice board with sticky tape

Once you have done this you can put a picture of the sun (Figure 6) and the moon or a bed in the left-hand columns.

Figure 6 The sun

A completed staff rota photo board is shown in Figure 7.

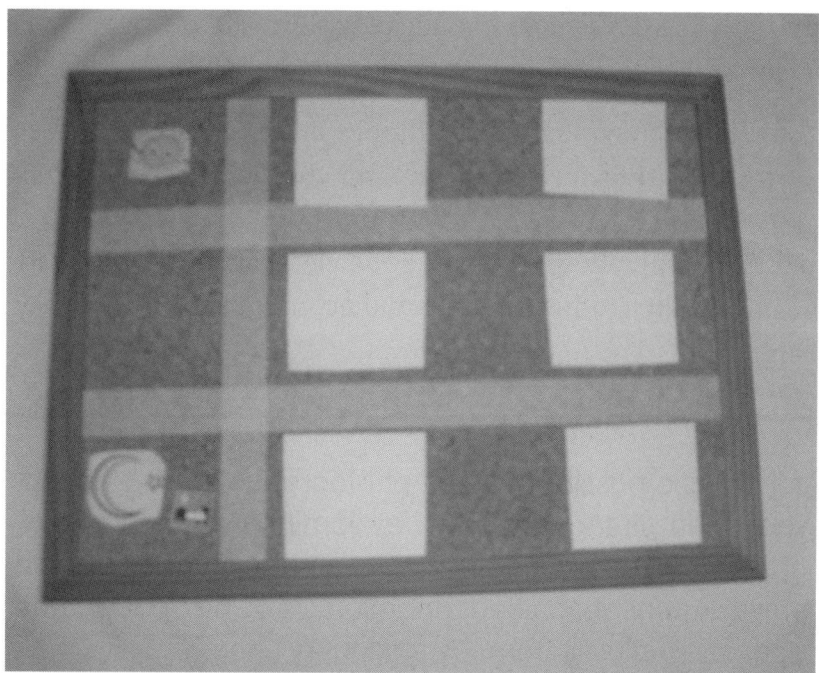

Figure 7 Staff duty rota photo board

You will see that I have put white squares in Figure 7: this is to show where the photographs should go. To start with you may wish to use sticky tape and later purchase Velcro and stick it on with glue.

- The top row will house the photos of staff who will be coming in for the early shift, the second row will be for staff on the afternoon shift and the third row will be for night staff coming on shift.

- At the bottom of the third row you may have room to put photographs of the service users who are currently in the building. When staff and service users leave the building to go to college, day service, shop, holiday, etc., the photographs should be removed and then replaced on their return.

- You may also wish to add times of shifts beneath the photos (e.g. 2–4p.m. or 7–3p.m.) to make these very clear. This will also add extra information about who is in the building.

- Once the service users come back from where they have been (e.g. college, day service, shop, holiday) their photos can be put back on to the board.

- If a member of staff is sick and the photographs have already gone up onto the board, you could put a first-aid plaster over part of the photograph to inform others that the staff member is unwell and will not be in.

- At the very top of the board you may wish to add the date each day (this is useful for people who cannot retain information for long periods).

The next step is to screw small picture hooks into the back of each side of the board and thread string through them and then it is ready to be hung on the wall.

Try to use photographs that show a good clear picture of each staff member and has no one else in it (otherwise this could confuse people until they get used to the board).

> If there is a possibility of the photographs getting ripped, you could strengthen them by laminating each photograph. If you do not have your own laminator, this could prove expensive; a cheaper option could be to buy some clear sticky plastic from the stationery shop.

You can use either drawing pins or Velcro on the back of each photo. Using sticky tape or Velcro on the actual board will be safer and will also save the photographs from being ruined by endless drawing pin holes.

'WHERE I WANT TO GO' PHOTO BOARD

You could have a big board on a wall with various photographs of local amenities, e.g. shop, park, library, bus, train, sports centre, cinema, theatre, and this will enable service users to point at what they would like to do or where they would like to go. They can also take the photo off the board and show it to you. This can act as a memory tool too.

You could use a similar board to that of the staff duty rota board (Figure 7) but it can be a bit limiting as it is framed and has square edges to it. You may like to try a more interesting design, perhaps something like a big map drawn on the wall which can be painted by the staff and service users.

Make sure you have enough room to space out the photographs, otherwise the individual may get a little confused or anxious if the pictures are too close together, e.g. if the picture of the shop and the picture of the dentist are right next to each other, what does this say to the individual? He will probably wonder if he is going to the dentist or to the shop.

MENU PHOTO BOARD

Service users will want to know what is for their evening meal. Why not devise a menu board and use pictures or photos so everyone can see what they are going to have? If they forget what is on the menu, they can always come back and have another look at the photo board. This will enable service users to be more independent, finding out for themselves what their evening meal is going to be. You could use the same style board we have talked about previously.

It can be difficult for some service users to say what they would like for their evening meal, or what they would like on the shopping list. One way to overcome this difficulty is to look through magazines and cut around pictures of meat, fish, vegetables, potatoes, rice, pasta etc. and when the shopping list is to be done sit with the individual at a table with these pictures and a dinner plate (use either a paper plate or real crockery).

Put the pictures into piles on the table. You will need meat in one pile, fish in the next, then vegetables, pasta etc. Move the meat pile next to the individual and ask him to choose what meat he wants then ask the individual to put the chosen meat onto the plate. Then ask him to choose the vegetable and follow the same process for the potato, rice, pasta etc.

Once the individuals have chosen items for the shopping list you can either put the pictures, fixed to a paper plate, onto the menu board or pin the individual items to the board, putting them in a circular shape so it represents the plate. You can do this for one evening meal or for the whole week. If you do the whole week, please ensure that each meal is compact and separate on the board. If it flows into the next meal, this can confuse service users.

GOING TO AND FROM THE SHOPS USING PHOTOS

Talking to a service user, you may want to say 'Would you like to get your coat and then we can go down to the shop and you can buy a magazine?' The service user, depending on his understanding skills, may understand all, some or none of this. Therefore, depending on the individual, you may need to use key words, e.g. coat, shop and magazine. If the individual doesn't understand verbal communication, then you can use pictures or photographs of coat, shop and magazine, ensuring that you show them in the order that you will be doing the task and say the words of what is in the picture.

Photographs and pictures can give a step-by-step guide to a whole activity being carried out. You could have individual photographs and pictures of coat, shop, magazine, book, chocolate, sweets, the place where the individual lives (to provide reassurance that he is coming back) and familiar landmarks, e.g. a telephone box or postbox that you might pass on your way.

For individuals who cannot take on too much 'memory', you can do a step-by-step approach, e.g. show or say 'coat' before you both walk out the front door, then you say or show the picture of the shop, you both start walking and once at the shop you say or show the picture of magazines and the person chooses the magazine. On the way back, show pictures of home or familiar landmarks, then return home.

If you have not got any photographs, start taking some. If you do not have a camera, it would be a good investment as photographs will help the people you support so much with their communication. The photographs can be placed in a photo album or pinned on a wall. If you know an individual is prone to ripping photographs or pictures, remember that you can laminate them or cover them in clear plastic.

To make a photo board that illustrates going to and from the shops, you could use the same sort of board as before. Remember to break the activity down into small chunks, e.g. if the next task is to get ready for going out, then the photographs on the board could show shoes, coat, scarf, type of transport he will be going in and the place where the individual is going, shops, college or day service, for example. Be very precise in the photographs you are using, e.g. if the person is due to go to the day centre or college, then make sure the photograph shows this, or if going to the shops, show a photograph of the various shops.

USING PICTURE BOOKS AND PHOTOGRAPH ALBUMS FOR ACTIVITIES OF DAILY LIVING

The contents of picture boards and photograph albums can be endless because as new photographs, pictures and activities are identified as being suitable, the boards/albums can be updated. This communication tool has no limits, but please do be careful that you do not overload the individual with too much information.

USING PICTURES AND PHOTOGRAPHS ON KITCHEN CUPBOARDS

This can enable service users to gain confidence in participating in their kitchen and have a visual reminder of where everything is. Some may choose not to do tasks for worrying about getting it wrong, as they don't know where anything is. For an example of how the service user may feel, think about when a friend of yours has just moved house and you are invited round for a meal and you offer to dry the dishes. How do you feel each time you say, 'Where does this go?' How do you think an individual may feel when he cannot ask, 'Where does this go?' Therefore, putting specific photographs on the cupboards will enable the person to be independent.

You may think that putting photographs on cupboards makes the kitchen look untidy. One thing to remember is that it is the service user's kitchen and if he has agreed that the photographs can go on his cupboards, then this is fine. Photographs and pictures can be stuck onto cupboards with a removable putty-like adhesive.

USING PHOTOGRAPHS ON SERVICE USERS' BEDROOM DOORS

Seeing their own photos on their door and knowing that they are going into their own bedroom and not going into someone else's bedroom can help service users to feel secure. It also prevents others going into the person's bedroom and potentially taking things that are not theirs. It also helps agency and new staff to know where the individuals are, especially when it is time for them to administer medication.

'WHAT I NEED TO DO WHEN I GET UP' PHOTO BOARD

We all need a structure to our day. Having a lie-in occasionally may be fine, but to have one every day is not good. If we do not know what we need to do when we get up, then this may cause us to stop in bed for fear of not knowing what to do once out of bed.

Many people can consult their diaries or remember from the day before what they need to be doing. However, for people who are unable to do this, but need their independence, you could devise a photo board which shows the individual each step of what he needs to do in the morning. Depending on the service user's ability to retain information, the sequence can be short or long.

You can illustrate each step, e.g. using the bathroom, using photos of the toilet, wash basin, shower, etc. You can have photos of the service user holding flannel and soap, then holding a toothbrush. Other photos could show the service user sitting at the dining room table eating breakfast. Once these tasks have been completed you can proceed to show the individual two shirts, two trousers, two jumpers etc. and ask him to choose from these.

USING PHOTOGRAPHS WHEN OUT OF THE HOUSE

You can put some photographs into a small pocket photo album and again use it to break down a task, e.g. if a service user is going to college by taxi, then the album could have a picture of the individual on the front of the album (so the service user can see it belongs to him and therefore includes him), followed by a photo of the front of the college, a photo of money (to remind the person to pay the taxi driver), a photo of the front showing the entrance door to the college , photo of the door of the room the individual needs to go in, perhaps a photo of the tutor, and so on.

Once the service user gets more confident in using photographs, you can both add more to the album.

> Don't forget to put the service user's name and the house telephone number in the album, so if the individual needs help, someone can ring you and let you know. You may wish to avoid putting the house address, just in case it gets into the wrong hands.

Alternative Ways of Communicating

TALKING PHOTO ALBUMS

These are a creative way of sharing information and you and the service user can use photographs, drawings, newspaper clippings etc. These are inserted into the sleeves of the photo album and you can record messages in a language of the individual's choice. The individual can press the play button on each page to activate the stored message. These albums are very versatile and can be used for many things, e.g. ordering in restaurants, making choices, talking timetable, shopping list etc. You can find them at www.inclusive.co.uk

CATALOGUES

These are good communication tools for the people you support. The individual can choose at home what he would like to buy, either from the catalogue company itself, or in the shops. Before buying it he can ask your opinion on it and if he is unable to go shopping, he can give you the picture and e.g. whatever measurements are required, and you can go and buy it on his behalf. Do not forget to get a receipt for the item.

FLASH CARDS

These are cards that have a picture on each card and will enable the individual to point to or pick up the card to show you what he would like to do or to eat, or what kind of support he would like. These can be purchased from ESL Flashcards: www.eslflashcards.com.

BROWN AND BEIGE PAINT CHARTS FOR CHECKING TEA AND COFFEE

We enjoy 'a good cup of tea' or 'a nice cup of coffee' and we all differ in how we like our tea and coffee made. Some say they like it strong, but what does that actually mean, e.g. only a little milk or using four tea bags? If the service user is unable to tell you how he likes his tea or coffee made, he can fetch the paint chart of browns and beiges and point to one colour. You can then write the individual's name on the colour piece in the paint chart and keep it in the kitchen so everyone can see it.

TURNING ON THE RADIO, CD, TV ETC.

If the service user is having difficulty remembering how to turn on the machine, or which button to press, you can ask the individual if he would like a coloured sticker put where he needs to press to turn it on and a different sticker to turn it off. If the individual is unable to express the colours of stickers to use, you could suggest a green sticker to start the machine and a red to turn it off. It is advisable to use the same colour stickers for each machine's controls.

TELECOMMUNICATIONS DEVICES

A telecommunications device for the deaf (TDD) can change letters typed on a keyboard into beeps and these can be transmitted over the telephone line. This communication tool can also translate into Braille and help people who are deaf-blind.

MOBILE TELEPHONES

There are many different mobiles, which vary not only in colour and size but also in key features. Here are some examples of key features that can assist people with communication difficulties:

- large screen, which helps individuals who have problems using the text

- orange backlight which is helpful for people with sight problems

- large buttons which will make it easier to press the correct buttons

- loudspeaker, volume control and powerful vibrations which will enable individuals who are hard of hearing to know they have a call or text coming through.

USING TELEPHONES

Some service users who cannot verbally communicate may still like to hear a familiar person's voice on the end of the telephone, or to ring to let the other person know he has got home safely. Some may be hard of hearing and need an amplified telephone. If the individual needs an amplified telephone, please ensure the controls are set so he can hear who is speaking on the other end of the telephone.

Some service users will need help to remember the telephone numbers of their family and friends. One way of helping is to make a telephone board. This can be a small notice board with photographs of the service user's family and friends, with their telephone numbers underneath (Figure 8 on the next page).

Another way of helping is to use a telephone like the one shown in Figure 9 on the next page. Small photos can be put in the spaces on the telephone to show important contacts. All the individual needs to do is press one of these photos to speak to his mum, social worker, friend etc. The telephone is programmed in such a way that the service user does not need to know the telephone number, all he needs to do is press the photo and he will be connected to the right person. You can find these phones at www.betterlifehealthcare.com

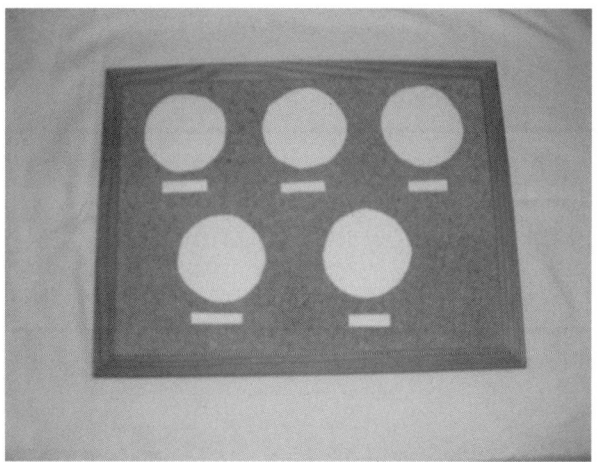

Figure 8 Telephone board

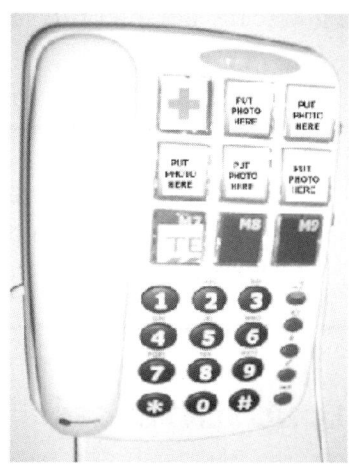

Figure 9 Telephone with pictures

VIDEO RECORDINGS

Using a video camera can be a good way of recording an activity and then showing it to the individual; this can provide confidence and raise the person's self-esteem. Sometimes the service user does not believe he can do a task (e.g. water the flowers in the garden) and by recording the individual doing the task it can be played back to him at a convenient time.

VERBAL COMMUNICATION

Remember to use the person's terminology, e.g. if the individual calls the midday meal 'dinner' and the evening meal 'tea' then you must call them by these names as well, regardless of whether you call the evening meal 'dinner' or 'supper'. If you do not do this, it can confuse the individual.

With some individuals, you can have a conversation and wave your arms (gesticulating) when you speak and perhaps laugh as well. For some individuals this will not be good as there will be too many distractions. Some people may prefer a straight face in factual conversation: simply give the information to the person so he can digest it. Some people are unable to digest facial expression, body language, jokes or emotions.

If an individual cannot talk, how will you know what he likes? Remember to watch the body language: someone who likes something will show it in many ways, e.g. the eyes light up, the eyebrows lift up when happy and lower when unhappy, sad or confused.

VOLUME

Some people from different cultures may talk more loudly than you and it can appear that they are angry. Tell them politely that you do not like it, do this in a quiet area where there are no other people; after all, you do not wish to embarrass the person. *Talk to and with the individual, not down to the individual. Do not shout, just be clear.*

> You may be tempted to finish off someone's sentence, but please do not do this as this can imply that you have no time for the individual.

USING LONG SENTENCES

The pace of the sentence should reflect the pace of the listener. Staff using long sentences can confuse or cause anxiety to some service users. For example, some individuals can understand a full sentence with different suggestions, commands and questions in it, e.g. 'Paul, go and get your coat and then we will go to the shop. What would you like to buy? A magazine or a book? What chocolate do you want to buy? Or would you like to buy some chocolate and a newspaper?' This is a very loaded, long question. Many of the people you support may become confused or anxious if you asked them this.

Have you noticed here that this example is putting ideas into Paul's head about what he should buy and therefore suggesting limited choices?

Paul will no doubt understand you are talking to him as you used his name, which is good practice, but if he has limited understanding or memory skills, he may only hear his name and the word 'go'. The result may be that he has gone (to wherever he thinks he needs to go) and now you have to go and find him.

✎ What could you have done instead?

. . . .

. . . .

. . . .

. . . .

WRITING LETTERS

Some individuals may prefer to write letters (sometimes with staff support) to family and friends and receive letters back. If they need any help with the content, they can give it to a staff member to read out.

Having one's own paper and envelopes in their bedroom can be a powerful tool for the individual. He can choose to write a letter when he wants to, rather than having to ask for some from the office and probably having to wait a while.

Some may like to receive text messages or emails (if the individual cannot read then the staff can help). The powerful tool here is that the individual is getting his *own* written message. If a relative rings to say he will visit this evening and the individual is out so cannot personally take the message, you could write it down and put it under the individual's door.

MAKATON

Makaton is a system of communication used with some people who have a learning disability. It consists of common and most essential key symbols and does not require the use of words; however, it is good practice to use the word along with the graphic symbol.

Some people will use Makaton to communicate. If an individual signs to you, sign back. This shows you are listening and confirms that the person is correct with his signing. This will give the person confidence and encouragement to sign more.

Some people may not be able to do the Makaton signs exactly as perhaps they should but it does not matter as long as it is similar and the individual can get his needs across, e.g. the individual may not be able to do the proper sign for toilet (right arm across to left chest and slowly stroke chest up and down with the middle finger of the right hand) and may instead tap his left chest to indicate toilet.

Correcting people when they have signed one way for a long time can cause the individual frustration and demotivation. As long as the individual can communicate to others and others can communicate with the individual, then this is fine. Rather than correct the individual, you will need to add to his care plan or communication profile that this is how the person communicates the need for the toilet.

> Everyone must work the same way and use the same communication approaches and tools to ensure that the service user receives consistent messages.

ACCESSIBLE INFORMATION

Information needs to be accessible to all service users. For example, if an individual has dyslexia he may prefer for information to be on a pale yellow background and written in a size 12 font. Each person with dyslexia is an individual and pale yellow may not be the best colour for another individual. You could try using coloured acetates to find out each individual's colour preference. Some individuals will need information broken down and you can use images to make the information easier to understand.

It is important for service users to be able to comment on the care and support they receive.

✍ Is your organization's policy or procedure for commenting on the care and support received in a format which the individual will find easy and quick to read?   Yes/No

If you answered no, what can be done to improve this situation?

. . . .

. . . .

Some individuals will need information broken down and you can use images to make the information easier to understand.

✍ Does each service user have his own copy on how to comment on the care and support he receives?   Yes/No

If you answered no, then what should be done about this?

. . . .

. . . .

COMPUTERS AND LAPTOPS

If the service user has access to a computer you can assess his ability to use it. If he cannot use it, you can ask if you can sit with the individual and point out which keys need to be pressed.

More computer ideas:

- if the individual can verbally communicate then he could get a voice-activated computer

- a minicom for service users who are deaf

- a computer with Braille

- ask the individual if he wishes to enrol in a computer class to learn to type or how to use email

- if the individual is unable to remember a password, he could purchase a plug in fingerprint-reader that accepts the individual's fingerprint as a password. These are available from www.m2sys.com

TAPE RECORDER

Some individuals, whether they can write or not, may like to use a tape recorder to speak to people (especially those individuals who are not confident in speaking but wish to get a message across) or to remember things.

For example, an individual would like to go shopping next week but does not feel confident to mention it. He could say it into the tape recorder and could then point to the tape recorder indicating he wants the staff to play it and listen to the message. He can also use the tape recorder to record his letter in the privacy of his own room.

HOW TO ENABLE OTHERS PRESENT TO KNOW WHAT THE INDIVIDUAL IS COMMUNICATING

It is important that the service user is present and participates in meetings that affect him, e.g. reviews or person-centred planning; if he can chair the meeting all the better. Some individuals you support may not be able to verbally contribute and you will need to consider other ways of enabling others present to know what the individual is saying when he is communicating.

Here are a few ideas:

- Purchase a talking photo album and record messages.

- Make up a scrapbook or photo album with the individual of his likes and dislikes, things he has done or achieved since the last review and take it to the review.

- Make a video of the individual doing things he likes or his achievements.

- Bring along a variety of things that shows what the individual has done, e.g. a pot he made in pottery, a folder that he bought ready for his new course etc.

SIGHT-READING

Sight-reading is when an individual has not learnt to read but has learnt to recognize some words. Some people therefore will not be able to read a sentence but will know some individual words. For example, when reading the word 'clock' the person may associate it with the clock on the wall.

SMELL

We may react to people based on their smell. Perfumes, aftershave and body odours can be an important way of recognizing people. People can associate these and other smells, e.g. meals being cooked, with events, e.g. mealtimes.

FEEDING

Some of the individuals you support may require help with eating and this can be helping the service user to use cutlery, being fed via PEG (feeding tubes) or actual feeding, and it is important that you inform the individual each time you are going to put food into his mouth. The individual's level of communication, including hearing and seeing, will determine how you do this.

Some people will need you to demonstrate, other than verbally, what you are going to do. A way of informing an individual you are going to put food into his mouth could be by:

- putting the spoon or fork into the individual's hand

- tap the individual's chin twice and then support the elbow to the mouth.

The person may take a while to understand what you are doing but after a while he will know. It is important that everyone does the same technique all the time, otherwise this could confuse the individual.

TOUCH

> Some people from different cultures may touch you more than you are used to. If you do not like it, politely tell the person.

Touch is one of our senses, and can be used to encourage communication. There are two types of touch, acceptable and unacceptable.

Acceptable touch includes the following:

- touching when it makes people feel comfortable to talk shows that you are listening, that you care, that you enjoy the person's company and that you like that person

- touching by professionals, e.g. when taking temperature or blood, or during physiotherapy

- touching by hairdressers, reflexologists, aromatherapists, shop assistants

- supporting someone's arm and guiding him across the road

- using the person's elbow to guide his arm to lift a mug and put it to his mouth

- putting your hand over the person's hand when helping him use a knife and fork

- tapping a deaf person on the shoulder to get his attention

- hugging people when we are happy (initiated by the individual)

- touching the arm when someone is upset

- touching the hand or fingers when teaching sign language or Makaton

- washing someone's hair

- shaking hands, but remember that in some cultures men will not shake hands with females.

Physical touch can be important to some individuals, but unacceptable to others:

- Some individuals do not like touch and can feel threatened by touch.

- They can feel their personal space is invaded.

- Touching someone can be culturally unacceptable if you are not a family relative or close friend.

- Touch could have a sexual implication.

- Someone may have been abused in the past and therefore wary of being touched.

- Staff members may be hugging inappropriately.

- Sexual touching with sexual intent is unacceptable.

- Many people with autism may well be hypersensitive to touch.

- Touching is unacceptable when it hurts, e.g. doing hand-over-hand support for someone to use his knife and fork where it hurts his hands, is unacceptable and you should stop the task immediately.

> We all need to be aware of touch, who is giving it and whether the other person wants it. You will need to ask the service user and/or check the care plan or communication profile to see if it says that the individual does or does not like touch.

Some organizations have clear policies on touch. Some say you can hug a service user if it is initiated by the individual, or you can comfort him by putting your arm around his shoulder if he is distressed. However, other organizations see this arm around the shoulder as a potential way of grooming the individual. Some organizations state very clearly that there should not be any touch apart from that when doing personal care.

✍ What does your organization's policy say?

. . . .

. . . .

How will you know if an individual likes touch?

You could ask the service user himself, his family, friends or advocate; you can also check the person's care plan, communication profile or passport. If the person does not like touch then it is important that this information is entered onto the individual's care plan, communication profile or passport (if it is not already on there).

Some individuals may receive 'touch' only when they have been using challenging behaviour and therefore receive control and restraint. Hands-on control can be used only if there is an agreed procedure in place and staff have received training. The result is that some service users have physical touch only when they have challenged and they challenge more to get the 'touch'. Therefore, we need to gently teach individuals that they do not need to challenge to get physical touch and comfort.

Making Choices

If the service user is not used to making choices then you may wish to offer only two items for the individual to choose from. This can be in the form of verbally asking the individual or showing two pictures or photos, and waiting for a verbal answer or watching the individual's body language; sometimes a wink or smile can let you know what the individual wants.

While out shopping recently I knew I wanted to buy a cake but had not decided which one. When I went into the shop and saw the numerous trays of cakes, I became a little overwhelmed as I had so many to choose from (and there was a queue behind, which caused me to be anxious). As the person behind the counter put her hands on her hips and again asked me what I wanted, I panicked and chose the nearest thing to me.

Is this the same for the people you support?   Yes/No

If you have answered 'Yes', what can you do about it?

. . . .

. . . .

. . . .

. . . .

Personal Space

The service user's personal preferences will determine how close he likes you to be when communicating with him: this is his personal space. It is important that you know the distance the individual prefers. Get it wrong and it can stop the person communicating; it can cause distress, discomfort and (for some people) fear if their personal space is invaded.

Space between people can differ and this will depend on the relationships we have. Most relationships involve what we call social space, which can be between four and nine feet (1.2–2.7 metres) and personal space between friends can be 18 inches to four feet (0.45–1.2 metres).

Personal space is very important and if you are too close to an individual, he could feel intimidated.

- *Intimate* distance: 6–24 inches (15–60 cm) is acceptable in close relationships.

- *Personal* distance: 2–4 feet (0.60–1.2 metres) is acceptable at social gatherings.

- *Social* distance: 4–12 feet (1.2–3.66 metres) is used when we are speaking to people we do not know.

- *Public* distance: over 12 feet (3.66 metres) is acceptable when addressing a large group.

If you are helping an individual with his personal care, then you will no doubt be entering his intimate zone. You must always ask if you can help the individual with the task and wait for an answer. If the individual cannot speak, wait for the reaction in the body language.

✍ Try these exercises with a colleague or a family member:

Ask him to stand close to you as though he is going to brush your hair.

How does it feel?

. . . .

. . . .

Ask him to stand close to you while you are sitting in a chair.

How does it feel?

. . . .

. . . .

Body Language

Body language can reveal a lot about the way a person is feeling. When giving information to another person, his facial expression will show if he is happy or not with what you are saying or doing. (Beware of cultural differences, e.g. in Japan a smile can mean one is embarrassed.)

Here are some examples of staff body language:

Female staff dressed inappropriately: e.g. wearing tight blouses or tops, showing cleavage, wearing tight short skirts showing shape of thighs, or revealing their thighs: staff should not be wearing this to work, but if one did, it could be interpreted as provocative and teasing.

Male staff dressed inappropriately: e.g. wearing tight or short shorts or not wearing a shirt: staff should not be wearing this to work, but if one did, it could be interpreted as provocative and teasing.

Standing with hands on hips, with shoulders back: this can be interpreted as you being unhappy or angry.

Pointing: this can mean two things: pointing to an object can mean you are hoping that the individual will follow your finger and look; pointing a finger at a person can mean that you are angry and having a go at that person or telling him off.

Nodding: this can mean the person is saying 'Yes'. (However, it means the opposite in Syria.)

Staring: directly staring at the individual, without blinking, can be interpreted as you being upset, angry or annoyed at him.

Subconscious actions: tapping of nails or feet can show you are in a hurry or irritable etc.

Not giving eye contact: if you are in the same room as someone else and do not have eye contact with the person you are speaking to, then you have not engaged with that person.

Giving eye contact: in English culture we are told to 'look at me when I am speaking to you' and therefore not giving someone eye contact can be interpreted as either you are not talking to the person, or you have no respect for the person.

When listening we need to:

- see the person's eyebrows move

- see the person's mouth and watch it move

- look into the person's eyes because they reveal so much. (Remember that a staff member wearing glasses can put an individual off talking to him due to not seeing his eyes, which can bring in fear or feeling scared).

We can lose a lot of understanding if we are unable to see facial expressions.

✍ Ask a colleague or family member to put on a pair of sunglasses and tell you what he did last night. He does not need to go into detail, just spend a couple of minutes talking to you.

How did you find the conversation?

. . . .

. . . .

. . . .

. . . .

✍ Ask a colleague or family member to stand near you and tell you what he is going to do tonight. Please ensure that neither of you have eye contact.

How did you find the conversation?

. . . .

. . . .

. . . .

. . . .

Some cultures are taught to show respect by not looking in the eyes when speaking, instead they may look down as a sign of respect.

Some may see eye contact (especially prolonged eye contact) as threatening and/or confrontational. Rather than look into the eyes when talking you could talk to the person's shoulder.

Standing with arms folded (crossed) and shoulders back: this is called 'closed body language' and can mean that either you are upset, angry or annoyed, or you do not really wish to communicate with this person.

✍ Ask a colleague or family member to stand by you with his arms folded across his chest while you tell him what you did yesterday afternoon or evening. No need to go into detail, just a few minutes talking.

How did you find the conversation?

. . . .

. . . .

. . . .

. . . .

Sitting with legs crossed (with the leg nearest to the other person crossed over the other leg): again, this is called 'closed body language' and by crossing your leg in this way you are 'blocking' the other person and your body is saying that you do not wish to communicate with him/her. Of course, it may be you are doing this without thinking; equally, a service user can do this without thinking.

✍ What is this woman's body language telling you?

. . . .

. . . .

. . . .

. . . .

Supporting Various Kinds of Service Users

SUPPORTING PEOPLE WHO ARE SHY

If the service user is shy, the worst thing you can do is to force the person to talk. What you can do is ask open-ended questions and wait for an answer. For example, an open-ended question would be 'How are you?' A closed question would be 'Are you OK?' To answer a closed question, the individual can say (or nod) 'Yes' or 'No'. Whereas if you ask an open-ended question then the person is encouraged to say more than 'Yes' or 'No'. The person may look at the floor or away from you, but this may not mean that he is not listening; it could mean that he is contemplating an answer. An answer may be a nod.

A person who is shy and/or who has low self-esteem may choose to hide behind sunglasses or a cap pulled down over his forehead. Do not ask the individual to remove the glasses or cap until he feels a little more comfortable being around you.

SUPPORTING PEOPLE WHO HAVE HEARING LOSS

A service user who has difficulty hearing will make communication difficult as the person may hear blurred conversation or none at all. Speak clearly and directly to the person so the person can read your lips. Do not shout as this will distort your face and lips and the person will read something other than what you are saying. Make sure there is no background noise when communicating.

You could arrange for flashing lights to be installed and connected to the front door bell. This will signal that someone has rung the door bell.

Does the individual wear a hearing aid? Is it working and is it at the right volume or pitch? Does it fit and does it improve the individual's hearing? Encourage the person to wear it. A build-up of wax can prevent a hearing aid working effectively; therefore, it is best to check that the ears are clear from wax.

> Some people who are both deaf and blind and use a walking stick will have two coloured rings on their walking stick.

SUPPORTING PEOPLE WHO ARE DEAF, HARD OF HEARING, AND/OR SPEECH-IMPAIRED

A minicom machine is a telephone typewriter device which translates the spoken word into a written message. This is a communication tool for communication between deaf, hard of hearing, and/or speech-impaired.

If the service user is unable to read the messages, he will need someone to read them to him. The person reading the message will have to speak clearly (so the individual can lipread) or have skills in sign language to translate the message.

Interpreters can be used and you can get a list of interpreters from your social services department. Please be aware that you cannot use an interpreter all the time.

SUPPORTING PEOPLE WITH A VISUAL IMPAIRMENT

If the individual is visually impaired, he will not be able to see your body language and pick up on the visual signals you are giving. This means that his reply to you may be different from what you were expecting to receive.

The service user will hear you and will also pick up on your scent (either perfume or body odour). Verbal communication is very important for people who are visually impaired and you need to introduce or announce yourself as soon as you enter the room or person's space. Remember to inform the person of every little step you will be doing while in the room.

Ask the individual how he would like to communicate. If the individual needs support to move around, please ask him how he would like you to do this. If he is unsure ask him to place his hand on your shoulder or your arm and ask him if this is OK.

A service can be designed to help the individual find his way around it and you will find some ideas under the heading of 'Environment factors' in this workbook, in the section on 'Factors affecting communication'.

> Some individuals who are blind may have a specially trained dog and/or a walking stick with a coloured ring on it. It is recommended that you do not stroke the dog as this could distract him from his responsibilities.

SUPPORTING PEOPLE WHO HAVE DEMENTIA

Dementia often affects older people and involves a decline in memory loss. Some have a short-term memory loss which means that a person may not remember something that happened or was said recently, but can remember things from the past.

You may have to repeat things often and this can be upsetting for you, but please remember that not being able to remember must be very distressing and frustrating for the service user. Be patient and if you do get frustrated, do not show it.

Communication skills of people who have dementia may differ from day to day. Individuals may experience difficulty in finding the right words to express their thoughts, have muddled thinking and/or problems remembering names etc. If they are in pain they will not be able to concentrate and may feel agitated.

One day the communication may be clear and the next day it may appear vague or inconsequential. When this happens you will need to pick up on phrases or key words that the individual seems particularly animated on and respond to these. After the individual has finished talking, you can repeat the words back to him to ensure you have the correct understanding.

SUPPORTING PEOPLE WHO HAVE A PHYSICAL DISABILITY

People who have cerebral palsy will hear what has been said and will make a decision in the brain, but will have difficulty giving a response as they will be unable to control the muscles that affect the voice. Therefore the words will not come out the way they should. The person will have difficulty finding the words to reply to you, therefore you will need to give time for a response.

Some people who have had a stroke will also experience the difficulties that a person with cerebral palsy has. They may have dysphasia, which means they are unable to express themselves as they cannot find the right words to use and may not be able to understand what is being said. Therefore you will need to:

- speak slowly

- refrain from using long sentences; use short ones, and using gesture and/or flash cards will also help

- give time for a response

- ask questions to ensure both of you understand the conversation.

SUPPORTING PEOPLE WHO HAVE A LEARNING DISABILITY

A learning disability can mean that the service user has limited ability to understand and process information. The ability to communicate and understand will depend on the level of learning disability that an individual has. Some may be able to understand what is being said and respond better than others. Many may have a short attention span and may require things to be repeated.

As each person has an individual level of learning disability, this means that the way you communicate will also be individual to that one person.

People with Down syndrome may have a large tongue which will affect their ability to speak clearly.

Remember to look at the communication profile or passport, which will enable you to gain a lot of information on how the individual wishes and needs to communicate.

Sensitive and Complex Issues

It can be very difficult for a service user to tell you something that is sensitive and complex and probably something that he has not told anyone else. This could be because the information is so sensitive.

✍ Take a little time here to think about how you would feel telling one of your friends about your sexual feelings? How would you feel telling one of your friends that your partner hits you or that you are feeling depressed?

. . . .

. . . .

. . . .

. . . .

✍ How do you think an individual feels telling you about his sexual feelings or that his partner hits him or that he is feeling depressed?

. . . .

. . . .

. . . .

. . . .

Service users can feel vulnerable after they have confided in staff. An example of this is if an individual has been abused and does not want to talk about it. It has to be reported and the individual will have to relive the incident by talking about it. By giving this sensitive information to the carer, the individual could feel vulnerable as the carer has confidential information about the individual.

Having knowledge can be powerful and informing others in the care team can help provide a consistent approach to care and support, but unfortunately it can be abused.

Here are some examples of sensitive and complex issues that you may need to discuss or pass on to the service user:

- His girlfriend has rung and says she does not want to go out with him any more.

- The service user is given news of a bereavement.

- A family member does not wish to visit any more.

- The service user is being abused by her father and you want to advise her not to go home this weekend.

- The service user keeps saying that her 'daughter put her in the home' and she wants to go back to her house.

- The individual is going to harm himself.

Whatever the issue, you need to ask yourself, 'Am I trained to discuss this with the person or is there someone more qualified to do so?'

Sometimes the individual will want or need someone experienced in the above issues to support him through it. Other times the individual may want to talk to someone like yourself who he knows reasonably well and trusts.

Please ensure that service users have the correct support to enable them to communicate their views and preferences.

You will need to ask if they want support from you and what type. If you give support without asking and they do not want it they could accuse you of interfering or you may give the wrong support, or too much so that they feel disempowered. You can guage what support the individual would like by asking. As you will have read previously it is best to ask open questions and in a private area, not in front of others.

There may be occasions when there is not enough time to ask what level of support the individual would like. For example if an individual is going to harm himself, you would follow his risk assessment or care plan and intervene or get help immediately.

Some individuals who have mental health needs and who could harm themselves have completed a risk assessment or care plan with the manager or community nurse saying something like 'If I harm myself in the future this is what I want you to do…' and it will have information there instructing staff on what to do.

When an individual is distressed his behaviour will change from what you are used to seeing. The changes that you may see are:

- The breathing becomes faster.

- The facial expression will be frowning or scowling and there is reddening of the face and neck.

- The body language may show the individual with his fists clenched.

You will need to record the level of support you gave and describe the incident if appropriate.

✍ Please ask your manager what you should do when you are faced with sensitive issues and write the answers here (including any forms you need to complete e.g. care plan):

. . . .

. . . .

. . . .

. . . .

Human Growth and Development

The development of people has been studied by many theorists, for example Maslow, Erikson, Piaget and Bowlby.

There are various models that can be used to see if an individual's needs are being met and one that I am going to use is the model of Abraham Maslow's Hierarchy of Needs. This is a theory in psychology that Maslow proposed in his 1943 article, 'A theory of human motivation'. As you can see, it has five levels to it, with the most basic needs at the bottom of the pyramid.

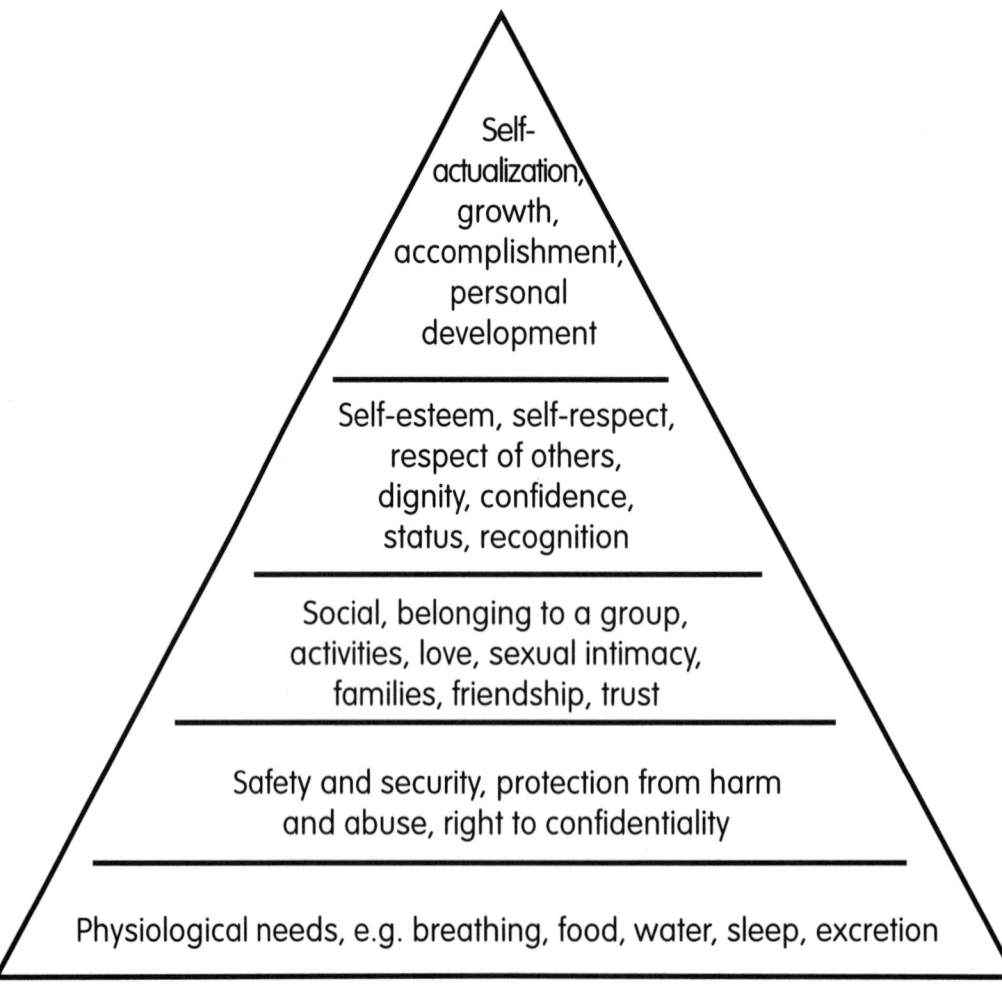

Self-actualization, growth, accomplishment, personal development

Self-esteem, self-respect, respect of others, dignity, confidence, status, recognition

Social, belonging to a group, activities, love, sexual intimacy, families, friendship, trust

Safety and security, protection from harm and abuse, right to confidentiality

Physiological needs, e.g. breathing, food, water, sleep, excretion

According to Maslow, until the two bottom levels are achieved, it is unlikely that a person can move on and develop. There will be some people who you support who may have achieved the majority or all of these stages and there may be some who have not. Therefore, you need to consider with each individual where they are at and how you can provide the individual with the right support to achieve the other levels and reach self-actualization (assuming these have not been reached yet).

✎ Looking at Maslow's Hierarchy of Needs, which levels are being met in your place of work?

. . . .

. . . .

. . . .

. . . .

HOW TO REACH THE HIGHER LEVELS

Personal development and growth: the service user needs opportunities to communicate and maintain skills and/or learn new skills and achieve. This can be anything from learning to prepare a snack, vacuum a carpet, swim, read or write, learn how to use the website, how to catch a bus, getting a job, chairing his own review, etc.

Status, recognition: we all need a role or two and when we carry out these roles people thank us and appreciate us. We all need to be able to communicate to decide what roles we would like.

✎ Think of an individual (call him 'Mr A') who lives in the service. What is your role in your house (where you live) and the individual's role where he lives?

Mr A's roles   My roles

. . . .

. . . .

. . . .

. . . .

If Mr A has not got any roles or responsibilities, you may wish to discus with him about bringing one or two in to start with if he is able to. They can be large or small, e.g. clearing the table after a meal or taking his crockery to the kitchen, or taking it in turn to chair the house meeting etc.

Social – belonging to a group: support is needed to enable the service user to be in a group (if he wants to). The individual needs to be able to communicate to decide what he would like to do. Examples of being in a group can be anything from doing voluntary work clearing woodland once a week, playing in a pool team in the pub, belonging to a book circle, being part of a club, going to bingo with a group of friends, attending reminiscence groups etc.

Social, activities, love and friendship: to enable people to find love and friendship, they need the opportunity to meet people.

Think of someone you support. What does the individual do during the day or the evening?

. . . .

. . . .

. . . .

. . . .

What would he like to do during the day or the evening?

. . . .

. . . .

. . . .

. . . .

What does the individual do during the day or the evening and who does he spend time with? We all need to have the opportunities to have friends and to be loved.

✍ Does the individual have these opportunities? Yes/No

If you have answered 'No', what are you going to do about it?

. . . .

. . . .

. . . .

. . . .

✍ How often does the individual invite family and/or friends round for a cup of tea?

. . . .

✍ How often does the family and/or friends have to invite themselves round for a cup of tea?

. . . .

✍ If the answer to the first question is greater than the answer to the second one, is there anything stopping the individual doing the inviting? Yes/No

Please explain your answer:

. . . .

. . . .

. . . .

. . . .

✍ Does the individual's communication level prevent him achieving the different levels and moving on?   Yes/No

If you have answered 'Yes', what can you do so that the individual can satisfy his higher needs?

. . . .

. . . .

. . . .

. . . .

✍ If the individual has not met all the levels of the hierarchy, how will this affect his self-esteem and independence?

. . . .

. . . .

. . . .

. . . .

How we dress and what we wear can have an effect on communication. Look at the following, what does it say?

✍ Staff always wear a suit at work: would you like to be supported by someone who wears a suit at work?   Yes/No

Please explain why:

. . . .

. . . .

. . . .

. . . .

✍ Staff come to work dressed as though they are going out to a nightclub or party: would you like to be supported by someone like this?   Yes/No

Please explain why:

. . . .

. . . .

. . . .

. . . .

✍ Would you like to be supported by staff who have keys hanging from their waistband?   Yes/No

Please explain why:

. . . .

. . . .

. . . .

. . . .

✍ Would you like to be supported by staff who have a tear in their clothes?   Yes/No

Please explain why:

. . . .

. . . .

. . . .

. . . .

✍ Can you think of anything else about a person's appearance that could affect that person's ability to communicate.

. . . .

. . . .

. . . .

. . . .

✍ Look at the service you work in and complete this table.

Question	Yes	No
Are the tables arranged so that when you and the service user communicate it feels like you are in an interview, i.e. do you have to sit across from each other?		
Does the environment need to be changed, i.e. walls are too bright or loud, rooms are cluttered?		
Is it noisy, e.g. staff talking loudly, TV on too loud, individuals running or shouting?		
Do the staff use a loud or aggressive tone of voice?		
Do staff mix with the service users or do they stay in one room and mix with the individuals only when a task needs to be done?		
Does the service have communication systems in place to enable the individuals to communicate or express their needs?		

✍ Now you have completed the table, what improvements need to be made?

. . . .

. . . .

. . . .

. . . .

✍ Observe a service user for a short while (no more than a few minutes). What is his or her behaviour and body language telling you?

. . . .

. . . .

. . . .

. . . .

✍ Observe a staff member for a short while (no more than a few minutes). What is his or her behaviour and body language telling you?

. . . .

. . . .

. . . .

. . . .

✍ Think of a service user and write how physical touch or contact can help him or her to communicate.

. . . .

. . . .

. . . .

. . . .

✍ Thinking of the individual you have just written about, please give two occasions when physical touch or contact is inappropriate.

1. . . . .

. . . .

2. . . . .

. . . .

✍ How can you encourage the service user you have been observing to communicate his or her needs?

. . . .

. . . .

. . . .

. . . .

✍ How can you encourage your colleagues to help this service user communicate his or her needs?

. . . .

. . . .

. . . .

. . . .

✍ It is important that everyone involved in the service user's life communicates the way the person needs them to. How can you encourage others, e.g. the day centre staff, family, friends, shopkeepers, milk person, to communicate effectively with the individual?

. . . .

. . . .

. . . .

. . . .

✍ How can you encourage the service user's family, friends, advocate and volunteer to encourage the individual to communicate?

. . . .

. . . .

. . . .

. . . .

✍ Is there a time when you would not encourage the individual to communicate? If 'Yes', please explain:

. . . .

. . . .

. . . .

. . . .

Recording and Reporting

Within your role you will need a range of skills to be able to respond to each individual. You will need to be able to write entries in care plans, write reports, complete charts, sign medication sheets and complete other documentation as required by your manager.

You will write down what you have been doing with the service user and if there are any changes in the individual's needs, e.g. if the person wears a hearing aid and the batteries are changed. You will also record if there any conflicts; an example of this could be that the individual refuses to wear the hearing aid and you should include what you did to resolve the situation.

You will also pass on things that worked well. It is important that this is written in the care notes so that others supporting the individual will read it and use the techniques you did. If you only pass it on verbally, it can be forgotten or not shared with others.

It is important that you report and record anything that concerns you and anything else that you have been asked to monitor and record.

Please refrain from using whiting-out fluid. If you make a mistake, put a line through it and initial it.

You are responsible for what you write and you should sign and date what you have written. This will enable others to refer back if needed and it can be used in court if needed. The person signing and dating the information is taking responsibility for what has been written.

Records are for you to read *and for you to write in.* If you do not record it, it did not happen.

A woman was admitted to hospital having taken an overdose. Her stomach was pumped and she was transferred to a mental-illness ward where she was diagnosed as depressive. She experienced delusions about Christ, snakes and fire. The registrar gave instructions that she was to continue to be nursed on that ward but that constant supervision was not necessary. Some days later, at the end of a visit, her husband handed the charge nurse a box of matches that his wife had said she intended to use on herself. The charge nurse did not record this in the patient's case notes. A few days later the patient went into the toilets with another box of matches and set fire to her skirt.

The trial judge in the case ruled that both the doctor and the nurse owed a duty of care. In the case of the doctor, the standard of care had not been breached, but in the case of the nurse this standard had been breached because any reasonably competent nurse would have recorded the incident with the matches.

(Aslangul and Meggitt 1996, p254)

Q: How much should I write? If I wrote: 'Joe was upset' would that be OK?

A: You will need to write more. When you are writing you are making a record of what happened. You need to give an accurate account and this will enable the rest of the team to read it and act on it if required. There may also be a need to refer back to it at a later date.

The records may be held on the works computer. Records on the computer should be saved in such a way that you or anyone else cannot delete any information either by mistake or deliberately. It is important that a computer is not left unattended while it is turned on.

Writing can be on a needs basis, e.g. when writing in care plans, for some service users you will need to write if they have had their bowels open and others who do not have a problem with their bowels will not need you to write this. Instead you may need to record their food intake or what they did during the day etc. Your manager will inform you on what needs to be written for each individual.

When you need to write something in a file or care plan you need to inform:

- someone that you have taken the file out of the cabinet to write in it. If the filing cabinet does not have dividers saying what each item is, then you may wish to put something in to mark the place where you took the file from.

- the service user what you are going to write and ask if they want to be with you when you write it or want it read to them once you have written it.

When writing you:

- must write clearly so other people can read what you have written

- should write only facts, do not write opinions

- must sign and date what you have written

- should use the spell check if using a computer.

It is important that you write only factual information. A fact is a reliable source of information. An opinion is a person's version of what he thinks happened or assumes to be true.

> A fact: it is raining today
>
> An opinion: I think it might rain today.

After writing in the care plan folder, you must return it to the secure area, e.g. office or locked filing cabinet if you work in a residential service. If you are working in someone's home, the person will have his own place where he would like to keep the care plan.

Confidentiality

Within your role you will be privy to a lot of information which is sensitive and confidential. You are being trusted not to tell people unless there is a reason to do so and, where possible, only when the individual has given their consent.

As a social care worker you must strive to maintain the confidence and trust of individuals and carers. This includes:

° Being honest and trustworthy

° Communicating in an appropriate, open, accurate and straightforward way

° Respecting confidential information and clearly explaining agency policies about confidentiality to individuals and carers

° Being reliable and dependable

° Honouring work commitments, agreements and arrangements and, when it is not possible to do so, explaining why to individuals and carers

° Declaring issues that might create conflicts of interest and making sure that they do not influence your judgement or practice

° Adhering to policies and procedures about accepting gifts and money from individuals and carers.

(General Social Care Council 2002, Standard 2)

There will be times when you need to share information with others, e.g. a general practitioner, a pharmacist, staff at the day service or in a hospital. You will need to tell the service user that you are going to pass on this information and explain why, e.g. continuity of care and support.

Some service users, e.g. some with a learning disability, may be unable to comprehend this and might think that they have done something wrong and this is why you are passing on the information.

Another example where you have to pass on information is where a service user has been harmed by someone or is going to harm himself; then you have to tell the person that you need to pass this information on. Sometimes service users will tell you something and say 'Don't tell anyone, it's a secret,' but you must tell the individual that you are not allowed to keep secrets and will have to tell someone.

You only need to pass on information which is relevant, e.g. the woman who works in the newsagent does not need to know that the individual did not sleep well last night, but the staff team do, and if the individual went to a day centre or college the following day then this information may be passed on to a key person there so staff can be aware that the individual may not have the same amount of concentration as usual due to being tired.

Q: If I go to the pub after work with someone I work with, can I discuss the service users then?

A: No. You are not allowed to discuss the service users outside of work with anyone.

Two examples of when confidentiality could be breached are as follows:

- When a family member asks about his relative: unless the service user has agreed to the relative having this information, you should not give it out. The family could argue that they have a right to know, but in fact, they do not.

- When a family member asks about another individual, e.g. 'How is Mrs Smith, my sister [service user] says she was sick last night.' It would be very tempting to reply saying how Mrs Smith is but you must not. All you can say is 'She is better now' or 'She is getting better.' To say any more would be breaking the trust of the individual.

Your company should have a policy on confidentiality which will incorporate the Privacy Act 1988. this Act governs:

- collection and protection of information

- how information should be kept or stored

- steps to take when urgent action is needed

- who will be responsible for deciding when information can be disclosed.

✍ Have you read it yet?   Yes/No

If you have answered 'No', please go and read it now.

What does the policy tell you?

. . . .

. . . .

Please tick the methods of communication you have in your workplace and write down how you can keep information confidential. If you do not know how to use email or anything else in the chart, please discuss it with your manager or supervisor.

Types of communication	Use in workplace? (tick)	How to keep it confidential
Face-to-face		
Answering the telephone		
Sending an email		
Sending a fax		
Care plans		
Records on the workplace computer		
Daily post		
Individual's review		
Handover sheets		
Records of supervision meetings		
Records of individuals' meetings		
Records of staff meetings		

Data Protection Act 1998

The Data Protection Act 1998 relates to personal information which can be held about an individual. It has rules that must be followed in terms of electronic and paper-based information and where and how individuals' personal information is stored.

The data should:

- be accurate and up to date

- be kept safe

- be fairly and lawfully processed

- be processed for limited purposes

- be available if the individual would like to see it

- be adequate

- not be kept for longer than necessary

- not be transferred to other countries without adequate protection

- not be sold

- not be disclosed to a third party who does not need to see it.

Everyone has a right to access information held on them and this includes service users asking to see what has been written about them.

The service user is not allowed to see any information that relates to him and another person: this information must be taken out so the service user cannot see it, unless the other person has agreed that the information can stay and the individual can see it.

The individual has a right to:

- be informed that records are held on him and why they are being held

- be informed of what the information is about and who has access to it

- have a copy of the information if he requires this

- be informed on how decisions about him have been made.

Access of Health Records Act 1990

Anyone over the age of 16 has the right to see his or her records unless there is a valid reason why this should not happen.

CODE OF PRACTICE

- Lock records away.
- Have secret electronic access codes.
- Do not discuss with those who do not need to know.
- Do not communicate information to those who do not need to know.
- Records should be handled only by authorized staff.

Self-Assessment Tool

✍ You have now finished this workbook. Please list below what you have learnt from this workbook and what changes you will make to your working practice:

. . . .

. . . .

. . . .

. . . .

✍ List below the areas of improvement that you need to discuss with your manager (if there are any):

. . . .

. . . .

. . . .

. . . .

✍ I now know:

What communication is   Yes/No

Why people communicate   Yes/No

How to support decision making   Yes/No

How to communicate   Yes/No

How the way we dress can be a form of communication   Yes/No

Barriers to communication   Yes/No

Different forms of communication   Yes/No

Variety of tools to enable individuals to communicate   Yes/No

How and why we need to record and report   Yes/No

Confidentiality   Yes/No

Signature of learner . . . . Date . . . .

Signature of supervisor . . . . Date . . . .

When you have completed this self-assessment tool, please do not worry if you have answered 'No' as you can go back and read the relevant sections again.

Certificate

. . . .

Name of company

THIS IS TO CERTIFY THAT

. . . .

Name of learner

Has completed training on

Effective Communication

ON

. . . .

Date

Name of Manager/Trainer . . . .

Signature of Manager/Trainer. . . . .

Name of workplace/training venue . . . .

Date . . . .

This is to be written on the back of the certificate:

This training has covered:

- Various ways of communicating
- Communication cycle
- Listening skills
- Factors affecting communication
- Personal space
- Body language
- Touch
- How communication can affect self-esteem and image
- Human growth and development
- Capacity to make a decision
- Communication profiles and communication passports
- Recording and reporting
- Storing of communication
- Confidentiality
- Communication within the team, with family and with outside agencies

Knowledge Specification Chart

WHERE TO FIND THE KNOWLEDGE SPECIFICATION (KS) FOR NVQ UNIT 31

KS		Pages
1	Legal and organizational requirements on equality, diversity, discrimination and rights: (a) relating to individuals' and key people's language and communication preferences (b) on equal treatment for language and communication (c) when completing records and reports.	10, 17 18, 91, 94
2	How to provide active support to enable individuals and key people to communicate their needs, views and preferences using their preferred method and media of communication and language.	18, 29, 31, 35, 40, 41, 44, 46, 55
3	Methods and ways of communicating that: (a) support equality and diversity (b) are effective when dealing with, and challenging discrimination when communicating with, individuals and key people.	18, 29, 31, 35, 40, 41, 44, 45, 55
4	Codes of practice and conduct; standards and guidance relevant to your own and others' roles, responsibilities, accountability and duties when communicating on difficult, complex and sensitive issues and recording and reporting.	10, 13, 17, 91, 94, 95
5	Current local, UK and European legislation and organizational requirements, procedures and practices for: (a) accessing records and information about an individual's communication and language needs and preferences (b) recording, reporting, confidentiality and sharing information, including data protection, communicating with individuals.	 13, 18, 91, 94, 95 13, 18, 91, 94, 95

6	Where to go and the best ways to find out about and get advice about individuals' communication and language needs, wishes and preferences.	18, 20
7	How and where to access information and support that can inform your knowledge and practice about communication and language skills.	18, 20
8	Theories relevant to the individuals with whom you work, about:	
	(a) human growth and development and its effects on communication and language skills and abilities	78
	(b) specific conditions in your area of practice that can affect communication and language of individuals and key people	23, 35, 71, 73
	(c) how communication and language differences and difficulties can affect the identity, self-esteem and self-image of the individuals with whom you work	38, 42, 43, 57, 71, 78
	(d) power and how it can be used and abused when communicating on difficult, sensitive and complex issues.	24, 36, 42, 76
9	Factors that can affect the communication skills, abilities and development of the individuals with whom you are working and any resultant behaviour that might occur.	23, 35, 73
10	Methods to support individuals to communicate.	29, 31, 33, 40, 41, 44, 46, 55
11	Specific aids to communicate that may be used in your area of work.	40, 44, 46, 55
12	How to arrange the environment and position yourself to maximize communication and interaction.	66, 68
13	Conflicts and dilemmas created by difficulties in communication and language in your area of work.	23, 71, 88
14	How to work with and resolve conflicts that you are likely to meet when communicating with individuals and key people.	14, 15, 18, 31, 88
15	The skills, styles and methods of communicating difficult, complex and sensitive messages and how to deal with the outcomes.	75

16	The environments that are most appropriate for communicating difficult, complex and sensitive messages.	75
17	Where, why and how to access permission to access records and reports.	18, 88
18	The difference between fact, opinion and judgement and why it is important when recording and reporting information about individuals.	88
19	How to and why you need to complete records accurately, completely and in ways that can be understood by those who need to access and use the records and reports.	88

Legislation and Useful Websites

LEGISLATION THAT COULD BE APPLICABLE TO THE PEOPLE YOU SUPPORT

Care Standards Act 2000
The Care Standards Act 2000 (CSA) provides for the administration of a variety of care institutions, including children's homes, independent hospitals, nursing homes and residential care homes.

Data Protection Act 1998
This Act protects the rights of the individual on information that is obtained, stored, processed or supplied and applies to both computerized and paper records and requires that appropriate security measures are in place.

Human Rights Act 2000
This Act promotes the fundamental rights and freedoms contained in the European Convention on Human Rights.

Mental Capacity Act 2005
This Act provides a clearer legal framework for people who lack capacity and sets out key principles and safeguards. It also includes the 'Deprivation of liberty safeguards' which aims to provide legal protection for vulnerable people who are deprived of their liberty other than under the Mental Health Act 1983. It is planned to come into effect in April 2009.

Mental Health Act 1983
This Act regulates the treatment of mentally ill people.

NHS and Community Care Act 1990
This Act helps people live safely in the community.

Safeguarding Vulnerable Groups Act 2006
The aim of this Act is to strengthen current safeguarding arrangements and prevent unsuitable people from working with children and adults who are vul-

nerable. It will change the way vetting happens and will be introduced gradually from autumn 2008.

USEFUL WEBSITES

All the following websites were accessed on 19 October 2008.

Age Concern

www.ageconcern.org.uk

Promotes the well-being of all older people.

Alzheimer's Society

www.alzheimers.org.uk

Leading the fight against dementia.

British Sign Language: Finger Spelling

www.british-sign.co.uk/fingerspelling

Gives information on how to spell words using hand movements.

Care Quality Commission

www.cqc.org.uk

CQC inspect and report on care services and councils. They are independent but set up by the government to improve social care and stamp out bad practice.

Change

www.changepeople.co.uk

Provides information in accessible formats, making information easier to understand.

Communication Matters

www.communicationmatters.org.uk

Communication Matters is a UK national charitable organization of members concerned with the augmentative and alternative communication (AAC) needs of people with complex communication needs.

Department of Health

www.dh.gov.uk

Providing health and social care policy, guidance and publications for NHS and social care professionals.

ESL Flashcards

www.eslflashcards.com

A fun way to increase vocabulary and improve spelling.

General Social Care Council

www.gscc.org.uk

Sets standards of conduct and practice for social care workers and their employers in England.

Inclusive Technology

www.inclusive.co.uk

Supplier of hardware equipment and software that helps people with special educational needs to use a computer, communicate and learn.

The Makaton Charity

www.makaton.org

Makaton uses signs and symbols to teach communication, language and literacy skills to people with communication and learning difficulties.

Mencap

www.mencap.org.uk

Mencap is the voice of learning disability and works with people with a learning disability to change laws and services, challenge prejudice and directly support thousands of people with a learning disability to live their lives as they choose.

Royal National Institute for Deaf People

www.RNID.org.uk

Changing the world for deaf and hard of hearing people. RNID is the largest charity representing the nine million deaf and hard of hearing people in the UK.

Royal National Institute for Blind People

www.RNIB.co.uk

National UK charity providing a good range of information for blind or partially sighted people.

Scope

www.scope.org.uk

Scope is a UK disability organization whose focus is people with cerebral palsy.

Speakability

www.speakability.org.uk

The UK 'voice' of people with aphasia, Speakability has a high-profile campaigning role and works to improve services for people with aphasia.

Valuing People

www.valuingpeople.gov.uk

Valuing People is the government's plan for making the lives of people with learning disabilities and the lives of their families better.

Widgit Software

www.widgit.com

Suppliers of educational and literacy software for pre-school, primary, special needs students and adults with learning difficulties.

References

Aslangul, S. and Meggitt, C. (1996) *Further Studies for Social Care*. London: Hodder & Stoughton.

Department of Health (2000) *Domiciliary Care: National Minimum Standards* (Care Quality Commission Communication Standard). London: Stationery Office.

Department of Health (2003) *Care Homes for Adults (18–65)* (Care Quality Commission Communication Standard). London: Stationery Office.

French, J.P.R. Jr, and Raven, B. (1960) 'The Bases of Social Power.' In D. Cartwright and A. Zander (eds) *Group Dynamics*. New York: Harper & Row.

General Social Care Council (GSCC) (2002) *Codes of Practice*. London: GSCC. Available at www.gscc.org.uk/codes, access on 19 October 2008.

Maslow, A.H. (1943) 'A theory of human motivation.' *Psychological Review 50*, 370–396.

Mehrabian, A. (1960) Professor Albert Mehrabian's Communications Model. Available at www.businessballs.com/mehrabiancommunications.htm, accessed on 19 October 2008.